Understanding

CLAUSE

AND

EFFECT

An essential key to
improving your writing

SUZANNE R. ROY

ISBN: 1496093550
ISBN-13: 978-1496093554

CONTENTS

INTRODUCTION   v

Part I: The Basics   11

Part II: Parts of Speech   25

Part III: The Subject/Verb Identification Process   51

Part IV: The Payoff   71

Part V: Punctuation   79

Part VI: Additional Things You Should Know   97

Part VII: The Payoff 2   115

CHALLENGE   127

CONCLUSION   129

   Appendix A   131

   Appendix B   133

   Appendix C   135

   Appendix D   137

ABOUT THE AUTHOR   145

INTRODUCTION

My purpose in writing this text is to provide you with enough basic elements of grammar and sentence structure to help you improve your editing skills -- that is, your ability to correct your writing so that the letters, reports, emails, and other written communications you rely on to get your ideas across to others are understandable and effective.

You will not find in this text a discussion of all the topics normally associated with grammar as a school subject, or a series of lists such as those found in standard grammar texts (except for a few short lists in Appendix A). Instead, I've chosen to focus on what I consider to be the key that opens the door to better writing – the ability to recognize subject/verb combinations – and have included only those elements that I believe you need to know in order to develop that ability. I believe that, once you've tasted the rewards that come to those writers who master the basics, you'll want to learn even more, at which point you can turn to traditional texts to meet your needs.

Because English is a complex living language, you will no doubt encounter constructions not addressed in this text. However, if you learn the process explained in the pages that follow, I'm confident that you'll be able to improve your ability to edit your writing without much difficulty.

This book is divided into the following sections:

In Part I:

- You'll learn some basics about sentences and clauses.
- You'll also get a preview of how an ability to recognize clauses can have a positive effect on your editing skills.

In Part II:

- You'll find a review of key parts of speech, with simple suggestions on how to recognize different types of words.
- You'll also learn which types of words can be subjects or objects and which ones can create objects. This new information will prepare you for what follows.

In Part III:

- You'll learn what is, in my opinion, the key to writing more effectively: how to identify clauses. Please take the time to learn the "Subject/Verb Identification Process" presented in this part of the text, even if you think you can recognize subjects and verbs in your writing. Once you master the process, I believe you'll see a marked improvement in your writing and editing skills.

In Part IV:

- You'll get a taste of the "payoff" that comes with mastering the clause recognition skill.

In Part V:

- You'll learn more about sentence structure and how to punctuate the clauses contained within the sentence spaces you create.
- You'll also review the elements of punctuation.

In Part VI:

- You'll discover additional ways in which your new skill can make editing easier.

In Part VII:

- You'll find additional examples of "clause and effect" in action.

Finally, in the Challenge:

- You'll be given additional opportunities to test your new skills.

You'll also find a few useful word lists in Appendix A, an abbreviated explanation of the Subject/Verb Identification Process in Appendix B, answers to the Punctuation Challenge in Appendix C, and the answers to the CHALLENGE in Appendix D.

Why I believe the key concepts that relate to "clause and effect" will work for you

I developed this approach to the teaching of grammar as a university writing instructor many years ago. To help my students understand why I insisted that they follow certain conventions of punctuation and syntax to improve their writing, I was forced to relearn grammar and to analyze it in a way I had never done before. If certain rules were not already clearly explained and justified in standard texts, I formed conclusions about their inherent sense in order to formulate my own explanations (with which not all grammarians will agree, I'm sure). This process allowed me to narrow in on and understand more completely those elements of grammar that have the most impact on the written expression of thought. It also led to my awareness of the critical value of clause-recognition skills as the single most important key to improving editing ability.

The resulting change in my own skills was amazing. Though I had long made a living as both a writing instructor and a writer, I saw my own editing abilities increase dramatically. That's why I'm convinced that you'll benefit from this approach, too.

A cautionary word about the writing process

It's important that you keep in mind that the writing process involves six steps: generating ideas, organizing them, writing a draft, stepping away from the draft, revising it, and editing it. This text obviously deals with the last step in the process: editing.

If basic grammar is to be of any value to you as a writer, its principles must be applied to your writing only AFTER you have committed your words to paper. To attempt to remember and follow the rules of grammar during the drafting stage is not only foolish but counterproductive and may actually interfere with the creative process. If you focus your energy on the task of getting your ideas down on paper during the first stage of the writing process and then allow yourself at least a small amount of time away from that first draft, you will be free to apply what you've learned in this text to the written words you have in front of you, and you'll discover that editing can be both fascinating and rewarding. Furthermore, once you've become adept at editing, you'll need to do less of it because you'll be so familiar with the rules that you'll follow them in the drafting process without being consciously focused on doing so.

<u>The key question</u>

Now that you know where I'm coming from in presenting the following material, here's a key question to ask yourself before you go any further:

- Does the quality of your writing matter to you?

If it doesn't matter, then don't bother with this book. If it does, please read on.

PART I – THE BASICS

The key to discovering basic choices in editing is to focus on the core elements of your writing – i.e., those elements that embody the basic message you're trying to convey. By improving your ability to recognize and understand those elements (namely, clauses, the subjects and verbs that make up those clauses, and the way clauses are linked and ordered within your sentences), you should be able to more easily determine whether:

- each subject is well chosen,
- each verb is well chosen,
- verb tenses are consistent and appropriate,
- the subject and verb in each clause agree,
- subordination has been properly used to vary the sentence structure and convey your intent,
- the sentences have been properly punctuated, and
- the message is as concise and forceful as possible.

Since your subjects and verbs embody the strength of your message, it is particularly critical that you learn to recognize and control these two elements.

My goal in this section is to give you some sense of how easy it is to edit writing when you understand sentence structure and can spot your subjects and verbs and the types of clauses in which they are found within your sentences. I should note here that, although the sample sentences used throughout this text may be simpler or less well constructed than the sentences you write, the principles remain the same and should allow you to look at your own work from a fresh angle.

Let's begin by reviewing basics about sentences themselves and about the clauses that are used to build those sentences. We'll deal with many of these concepts again as we go through the text, so absorb as much as you can and just let it sink in.

Sentences

<u>What exactly is a sentence?</u>

Teachers usually tell us that a sentence is a group of words that expresses a complete thought. Although this definition applies more specifically to an independent clause (that is, a subject/verb combination that expresses a complete thought), it is commonly applied to a sentence because a complete sentence must contain, at a minimum, one independent clause.

The problem with the definition is that people sometimes write sentences that don't express complete thoughts. Teachers may label these sentences "fragments," but readers still interpret them as sentences because they identify sentences by their appearance, not by their content. Sentences have a particular look that is typographical. For this reason, before we can talk about the content of a well-constructed sentence, we must consider its physical appearance on the page.

The space a sentence occupies

Think of a sentence first and foremost as a group of words occupying a specific physical space on your page. That space is marked off by a capital letter at the beginning and a period or other ending punctuation (question mark or exclamation point) at the end. For example, the space the previous sentence occupies is the area between the capital "T" and the period after the word "end."

Why should you bother to think in terms of the space the sentence occupies?

- For one thing, without a beginning capital and some sort of ending punctuation, you don't have a conventional sentence because no space has been defined for it. You merely have words or clauses dangling on your paper. Ignoring the typographical nature of the standard sentence may be fine for poetry or verse, but it is bound to interfere with your message in prose.
- Knowing about sentence space should also make you aware of the need to choose wisely what you put into that space, recognizing that it is a limited area in which the reader will expect to find at least one understandable and complete thought.
- When, as a reader, you recognize the space, you're more prepared to analyze its content and its effect on you, as well as its legitimacy as a complete thought.
- Finally, when you think of a sentence as a group of words confined within a limited space, you're more likely to understand why the rules of punctuation exist and how they can best be used to regulate words within

that given space. We'll learn more about sentences in a later chapter.

Fragments

A sentence fragment is just what it implies – a piece of sentence. You create a fragment when you fail to include at least one independent clause within the sentence space you've defined. Sometimes you might include one or several dependent clauses within the space; sometimes you might include only phrases (that is, groups of words that don't include a subject/verb combination) or even just a single word. In almost all cases, you've created a fragment. (I say "almost" because a sentence like "Speak!" is a complete sentence even though it contains only one word since it does contain an independent clause: Subject = [*You*]; verb = *speak*.)

What's wrong with fragments?

Nothing, when used sparingly and judiciously. In fact, they can be quite effective if they're used wisely for specific purposes. [Did you notice that the first sentence space in this paragraph contains a fragment?] However, if overused, they lose their effectiveness and can weaken or destroy your message. Furthermore, they have the potential of confusing or misleading readers, who tend to assume that anything within a sentence space represents a complete thought. As a reader, you should be aware that fragments are often used in advertising and in propaganda to sell "notions" that are not solid or credible enough to be expressed as complete ideas.

Remember: Sentences are the conventional means of communicating ideas in written English. Whether we realize it or not, we've learned to expect to find complete thoughts within sentence spaces.

Clauses

A clause is a group of words that includes a subject/verb combination (as opposed to a phrase, which is a group of words that work together that does not include such a combination).

Here's a sample sentence that you'll encounter several times in this text because it is simple yet allows for illustration of several key points I'd like to make about editing:

- *The car that was towed out of the parking lot belonged to Paul.*

In this sentence, "*The car belonged to Paul*" and "*that was towed out of the parking lot*" are two clauses. The subject/verb combinations are "*car*" [subject] and "*belonged*" [verb] in the first clause, and "*that*" [subject] and "*was towed*" [verb] in the second. Notice that "*out of the parking lot*" is simply a phrase – that is, a group of words that work together that does not include a subject/verb combination.

- A clause must have at least one working verb but may have more than one working verb.

The working verb of a clause – that is, the verb that expresses the action or state of being you're trying to convey – may be a single verb, a verb and its auxiliary (usually forms of the verbs *"to be"* or *"to have"*), or a series of verbs linked by commas and/or a coordinating conjunction (*or, for, nor, and, so, but, yet*).

In our sample sentence, each clause has only one working verb.

- A clause must also have at least one subject – that is, the person, place, thing, idea, or experience that is the focus of your message – but may have more than one subject linked by commas and/or a coordinating.

The main subject of the sentence is the subject of an independent clause within the sentence.

- The main subject is normally, though not always, the first significant noun or pronoun in the sentence.
- The subject may be hidden, as when a command is given (e.g., *"Move!"*). The subject *"you"* is silent but understood whenever you give such a command.

In our sample sentence, each clause has only one subject.

We'll talk more about subjects and verbs later in this section.

Structure of clauses

The normal structure of a clause in English is

- subject (+ modifiers) + working verb (+ modifiers) + object or predicate, if any (+ modifiers)

Even in complex sentences such as our sample sentence, where one clause is sometimes interwoven with another (notice how the second clause *"that was towed"* is found in the middle of the first clause, between the subject *"car"* and the verb *"belonged"*), the basic order of each clause usually remains intact.

NOTE: This normal structure is reversed when the sentence is a question, as you can see in the following example, where part of the verb precedes the subject:

- *Was the car towed today?*

Types of clauses

While there are many types of phrases, usually named for the initial word in the phrase (e.g., noun phrases, participial phrases, or prepositional phrases), there are only two types of clauses: independent clauses and dependent (sometimes also referred to as subordinate) clauses.

In discussing these two types of clauses, let's look at the example we used earlier.

- *The car that was towed out of the parking lot belonged to Paul.*

Independent clauses

- Unless the sentence has been inverted, the first subject in a sentence is usually part of an independent clause.
- An independent clause is not subordinated (that is, made secondary) to any other idea, though it may sometimes require one or more dependent (subordinate) clauses to complete its meaning.
- A thought expressed as an independent clause will be interpreted as a main idea within the sentence.

In the sample sentence, "*the car belonged to Paul*" is an independent clause.

- There is no indication that the sentence has been inverted, so the first subject in the sentence (*"car"*) is part of an independent clause. When we look to see what is being said about the car, we discover the verb that relates to car: it *"belonged"* to Paul.
- This subject/verb combination (*"car belonged"*) is not subordinated to any other idea, either by wording or by intent.
- The independent clause is meant to express the main idea in the sentence.

Dependent (or subordinate) clauses

- A dependent clause is usually recognizable because it begins with a subordinating term (i.e., a subordinating conjunction such as *"because"* or *"if"* or a relative pronoun such as *"that"* or *"which"*), although relative pronouns are sometimes suppressed or omitted.

- A dependent clause cannot stand on its own as a complete sentence, although sometimes the omission of the subordinating term that connects it to the main clause makes it seem as if it could stand by itself.
- Most important is the fact that a subordinating clause performs a specific function (subject, object, modifier) in relation to the main clause in the sentence or to one of that clause's elements and is, therefore, in a secondary or subordinate position to it.

In the sample sentence, *"that was towed out of the parking lot"* is a dependent clause.

- It begins with the subordinating relative pronoun *"that."*
- It cannot stand on its own as a complete sentence (in other words, you couldn't walk up to a person on the street and blurt out *"that was towed out of the parking lot"* and expect the person to perceive that as being a complete thought).
- It performs a function in the sentence – in this case, it modifies the subject of the main clause (which car? the car that was towed) – and is, therefore, in a secondary or subordinate position to the main idea.

That was a lot to take in, so let's look at another example to reinforce these concepts:

- *I am in hopes you will grant approval of my project.*

In this sentence, *"I am in hopes"* is an independent clause.

- There is no indication that the sentence has been inverted, so the first subject/verb combination in the sentence (*"I/am"*) is part of an independent clause.
- This clause is not subordinated to any other idea, either by wording or by intent.
- It is meant to express the main idea in the sentence (i.e., "I am" in hopes of something).

In the sentence, "[that] _you_ _will grant_ approval of my project" is a dependent clause.

- This clause should begin with the subordinating relative pronoun "*that,*" but the pronoun has been suppressed.
- This clause cannot stand on its own as a complete sentence (in other words, you couldn't walk up to a person on the street and blurt out "*that you will grant approval of my project*" and expect the person to perceive that as being a complete thought), and
- It performs a function in the sentence – in this case, it is meant to be an object (in hopes of what? that you will grant approval of my project) – and is, therefore, in a secondary or subordinate position to the main idea.

Effects

Now, let's see how the ability to spot clauses can help you to question your writing in a way that allows you to create different effects with the sentences you structure.

Staying with our first sentence – "*The car that was towed out of the parking lot belonged to Paul*" – we have spotted two clauses within the sentence space: (1) The independent clause "*The car belonged to Paul*" and (2) the dependent clause "*that was towed out of the parking lot.*"

Question #1:

Since you now know that the independent clause is meant to express the main idea behind your message, you can ask yourself if you really meant to focus on the fact that the car belonged to Paul.

Choices:

- If that is where you want to focus, then you know you are hitting the mark and can choose to leave the sentence as it is.
- If you really meant to focus on the fact that the car was towed away, then you know you'll have to shift the ideas around in terms of the types of clauses in which those ideas are found.

Let's assume that you did want to focus on the action. The new sentence would read as follows:

- *The car that belonged to Paul was towed out of the parking lot.*

Question #2:

If this revised sentence is what you choose, you can now ask yourself if the dependent clause could be stated more simply since it merely reflects a state of being and its only purpose appears to be to describe the car. (In a later chapter, we'll discuss the use of clause recognition to achieve conciseness in your writing.)

Choices:

- You could reduce the dependent clause to a phrase by eliminating the subject/verb combination and simply using a verbal: *The car belonging to Paul was towed out of the parking lot.*
- You could make the sentence even more concise by reducing the dependent clause to a single possessive noun: *Paul's car was towed out of the parking lot.*

The point I'm making here is that an ability to spot clauses is critical to creating the effect you intend when your write. You can quickly change both the focus of your message and the quality of your sentences if you know how to spot and use clauses. If clause recognition can have an effect on such a relatively uncomplicated sentence as the one above, imagine what it could lead to if applied to the more complicated sentences you write every day.

Let's try it again, just to reinforce the message.

In the second sentence -- *I am in hopes*[that] *you will grant approval of my project* – we've spotted two clauses: (1) The independent clause "*I am in hopes*" and (2) the dependent clause "[that] *you will grant approval of my project.*"

Question #1:

Looking at both clauses, ask yourself what you meant to focus on as your main idea.

Choices:

- If you want to focus on your hopes in order not to be too direct with the person being addressed, then you know you are hitting the mark and can choose to leave the sentence as it is.
- If you want to deliver a strong appeal to the reader, then you know you'll have to make the idea expressed in the dependent clause the focus of your sentence.

Question #2:

Once you've decided what effect you want to have on your reader, you can ask yourself how best to word your message so that it is as clear and effective as possible. As you consider this question, remember that English, which is largely based on Anglo Saxon, is most forceful and effective when you rely heavily on well-chosen verbs that represent actions rather than states of being. (In a later chapter, we'll discuss how to find and select the best verbs for the clauses you write.)

Choices:

1. If you've chosen to make the appeal as strong as possible, you will eliminate the first clause and turn the second clause into an independent one: *Please grant approval of my project.* Once you've done that, you can focus on the real action you are asking for, and you'll end up with an even stronger appeal: *Please approve my project.*
2. On the other hand, if you've opted to keep the message less forceful, you will leave the sentence as it is.

However, keeping in mind that the independent clause should, if possible, reflect an action rather than a state of being, you will focus on the real action in that clause and strengthen the message without being too direct, and then do the same for the dependent clause: *I hope you will approve my project.*

Again, please notice how such simple corrections can make your writing more direct and more concise. These are only a few of the choices that an ability to recognize clauses can help you to discover and use to improve your writing.

<u>Let's stop here</u>.

Before I give away all the editing secrets this text holds, let's get to work in developing the skills that will allow you to take full advantage of "clause and effect." Please take the time to go through the next few chapters, even if you think you already know the information or if you are normally put off by new processes. The results should surprise you.

PART II: PARTS OF SPEECH

Why should you know the parts of speech?

In other words, why should you be able to identify a pronoun or a preposition, a subject or a verb?

- The answer to this question is simple if you understand that (1) language is process, (2) process involves tools and materials, and (3) the parts of speech are the tools and materials you use to involve yourself in the language process.

If you don't understand this idea of process, think of any skill you have developed. Let's say that you like to do carpentry. As a child, perhaps you imitated a relative who liked to work with wood. You learned some basics – for instance, the difference between a hammer and a saw – strictly by observation. However, if the person you were watching held or used the saw the wrong way, you probably learned that, too. Could you now correct this mistake without learning how a saw is really meant to be held or used? Could you make progress in woodworking without understanding the different types of tools at your disposal? Could you hope to perfect your skill without understanding the different things you can do with a saw or a planer or any of the other tools you use? Could you even discuss the process without being able to name your tools? Probably not. To the extent that your understanding of the tools you use is limited, so is your ability to master your craft.

Why should developing skill in language be different from developing any other skill? When you first learn to speak, no one names the tools; you learn by imitation. However, you imitate the mistakes as well as the correct usages you hear. You can never learn to improve your speech unless you understand the tools you're working with and how they are meant to function.

When you learn to write, the process becomes even more complicated because it becomes visual. You must be able to identify not only the parts of speech but the punctuation marks you are going to use to organize and manage these words on paper. Any discussion of effective writing is virtually impossible if you don't know the names and functions of these tools.

- There is a second reason, however, why I've included a review of the parts of speech in this text.

As you've gathered by now, it is my belief that an ability to recognize clauses is central to your ability to edit and refine your work.

It is also my belief that, in order to develop that critical ability, you must be able to recognize words that can either (1) function as subjects or objects or (2) create objects (that is, be object-creators).

I'll explain this concept in the next chapter. For now, I encourage you to review the material that follows, paying particular attention to the subject/object and object-creator functions of each type of word. Read the examples, even if you think you already know how to identify these words. The knowledge you gain or solidify here will serve as an important building block in improving your writing ability and your editing skills.

Nouns

As you may recall from elementary school:

- Nouns are words that represent people, places, and things. You must also add to this list "ideas" since concept words such as *liberty* and *freedom* are nouns even though they do not represent people, places, or things.
- Nouns are normally in the third person and may be singular or plural.
- **Nouns can function as subjects or as objects within a sentence**

What you may never have been told, however, is that:

- **Nouns cannot create objects.** Please keep this in mind as you go through this text.

There are three types of nouns you are likely to run into:

- Common nouns – These are everyday nouns, the largest class of nouns you'll use.
- Proper nouns – These name specific people, places, etc., and are capitalized (your own name is a proper noun).
- Collective nouns – These represent a collection of people or things (e.g., *"class"* represents all the students within the class; *"jury"* represents the 12 people who make up the group).

If you have difficulty recognizing nouns, remember:

- Nouns can usually be preceded by: (1) articles (*a, an, the*), (2) pronouns that function as adjectives (e.g., *my, your, his, our, that* – as in "*that hat*"), and (3) regular adjectives (e.g., *beautiful, angry*, etc.).
- If the word you are looking at can represent a person, place, thing, or idea on its own without help, it is probably a noun.

Example:

- *Another <u>thing</u> I like about <u>Spring</u> is that the <u>sand</u> and <u>dirt</u> on the <u>roads</u> are gone, along with all the dirty snow <u>banks</u>.*

In this sentence, all of the underlined words are nouns. You can test this by adding "*the*" in front of each word.

NOTE: Nouns can serve as modifiers and thus become adjectives when (1) they immediately precede another noun which they describe or modify (like the word *snow* in the example above) or (2) they are part of a phrase that has been set off by commas and that describes or modifies the noun or pronoun that immediately precedes the phrase.

For example, in the sentence "*The circus troupe has arrived,*" "*circus*" immediately precedes and modifies "*troupe*" and cannot function as a noun. In the sentence "*My neighbor, a good friend, deserves praise,*" the word "*friend*" is part of a phrase that has been set off by commas (i.e., it is set in apposition to) and immediately follows and modifies "*neighbor*" and cannot function as a noun because it has become an adjective.

Pronouns

Pronouns are words that are used to replace nouns to avoid unnecessary repetition.

As you may remember from school:

- Real pronouns stand on their own -- that is, they are followed immediately by verbs, phrases, or clauses but not by nouns. [Don't mistake words like *my*, *your*, or *our* for pronouns; these words are usually followed immediately by nouns and really serve as adjectives that modify those nouns.]
- Pronouns can be classified as 1st, 2nd, or 3rd person and can be singular or plural.
- **Pronouns can function as subjects or as objects within a sentence.**

What you may never have been told, however, is that:

- **Pronouns cannot create objects.** Please keep this in mind as you go through this text.

There are several types of pronouns, not just the personal pronouns (*I, you, he*...) that probably come to mind when you think of pronouns.

In reviewing the list in Appendix A, pay particular attention to relative pronouns (*that, who, which*, etc.). We'll talk more about these pronouns when we discuss clauses.

If you have difficulty using pronouns, remember:

- A pronoun should not be used until the word it represents (i.e., its antecedent) has been used.

Example:

The voters were confused by the wording on the ballot. This led to interesting results.

In this sentence, *"this"* is a pronoun with no antecedent (that is, there is no single noun to which it refers). The word *"confusion"* should have been used instead:

Correction:

The voters were confused by the wording on the ballot. Their confusion led to interesting results.

- A pronoun should not be used if its connection to its antecedent may not be clear to the reader.

Example:

Tom reminded Jim that he was only five years old when their father died.

In this sentence, *"he"* could refer to *"Tom"* or to *"Jim"* since both are masculine singular words referring to a person. For clarity, the real antecedent should be repeated.

Correction:

Tom reminded Jim that Jim was only five years old when their father died.

- A pronoun can be used repeatedly as long as the connection to its antecedent is unbroken.

Example:

Michael was in a good mood. He had just won the game, and he couldn't wait to play another. Without hesitation, he urged his wife to refill the glasses, and he invited his friends to ante up. He knew this was going to be his night.

Correction: None required.

About "-self" pronouns

Pronouns ending in "-self" are reflexive in nature. These pronouns should not be used except in the following instances:

- The action in the sentence is directed at or reflected back to the subject of the sentence.

Example:

I hurt myself.

In this sentence, the hurting is directed back to the subject *"I"*.

- The subject wants to emphasize personal involvement in something. In this case, the pronoun is placed in apposition to the subject – that is, it is set off by commas and cannot operate either as a subject or an object.

Example:

I, myself, saw the accident.

NOTE: Sentences such as *"He spoke to Tom and myself about the accident"* or, worse still, *"Tom and myself heard about the accident"* are incorrect and should read *"He spoke to Tom and me about the accident"* or *"Tom and I heard about the accident."*

Remember: If you choose NEVER to use a "*-self*" pronoun, your decision will be correct 99% of the time.

Working Verbs

As you may remember from school:

- Words that serve as verbs within a sentence are the words that represent the actions or states of being at the core of the message.
- **Verbs that represent action can usually create objects.**
- **Verbs that represent states of being usually cannot create objects.** In most cases, they serve as mirrors or equals signs, which means that their "objects" equate with the subject. Such "objects" are really in the subjective case, not the objective case, and for our purposes are not true "objects."

What may never have been pointed out to you is that:

- **Working verbs cannot function as subjects or objects.**

If you have trouble recognizing working verbs (that is, verbs that serve their natural function within a sentence, as opposed to verbals that serve as nouns or adjectives), apply this simple two-pronged test:

- Try using personal pronouns with the verb without changing the rest of the sentence, AND
- Check to see if you can change the verb's tense without destroying the sentence. (Note: If the clause is a command, be sure to use the hidden "you" as you change the verb tenses. For example, "[You] speak!" would become "[You] spoke!" and "[You] will speak!")

Example:

The cats prance each night before the fire.

In this sentence, the word *"prance"* represents an action. To be sure it's a working verb:

- Apply personal pronouns to it.

I prance each night..., you prance each night..., he prances each night...

That works.

[Notice that you can't apply personal pronouns to a non-verb. For instance, you couldn't say "I night, you night, he nights" or "I because, you because, he becauses." That would be senseless.]

ALSO

- Check to see if you can change the verb's tense without destroying the sentence.

The cats will prance each night ... (future tense), *The cats pranced each night ..* (past tense)

The word passes both tests. Therefore, it is a working verb in the sentence.

Example:

The old man was tired and sick.

In this sentence, the word *"was"* represents a state of being. To be sure it's the working verb:

- Apply personal pronouns to it.

I was tired..., he was tired...

- Now change its tense.

The old man will be tired ... (future tense), *The old man is tired* ... (present tense)

Again, the word passes both tests and is, therefore, a working verb.

Note: Whenever a form of the verb "*to be*" (like *is, was, were, had been*) is used with a word that might be a verb, you must determine whether the passive voice is in use or whether the verb "*to be*" is meant to stand by itself. You can do this by checking to see whether the writer seemed to imply that the action was done by someone not focused on in the sentence.

In the example above, the word *"tired"* could represent the verb "*to tire*." However, it's obvious that the writer intended simply to describe the old man's state of being and not to imply that someone or something specific tired the old man out. For this reason, the working verb is simply *"was,"* not *"was tired."*

On the other hand, in the following sentence, the writer's intent is different:

The man was exhausted by the child's incessant demands.

In this sentence, the writer's intent is to say that the child's demands exhausted the man. This sentence is not merely descriptive; it focuses on an action "by" someone but is in the passive voice since the subject *"man"* is not the doer of the action. The verb is *"was exhausted"* and not simply *"was."* [We'll discuss "voice" at greater length later in this text.)

Verbals

Verbals are words that are derived from verbs but that are not meant to be working verbs within a sentence. They usually function as nouns or as modifiers instead.

There are three types of verbals you are likely to run into:

- Gerunds – These verbals end in "-ing" and usually serve as nouns or adjectives in the sentence.
- Participles – These verbals end in "-ed" and serve only as adjectives.
- Infinitives – These verbals usually include the word "to" and can serve as nouns, adjectives, or adverbs.

In all three cases, you can tell that they are not working verbs because they cannot pass the two-pronged test that working verbs always pass:

- You cannot apply pronouns to them without changing the rest of the sentence, AND
- You cannot change their tenses without destroying the readability of the sentence.

Gerunds

Gerunds are verb forms that end in "-ing."

- **Gerunds used as nouns can function as subjects or objects.**
- **Gerunds can create objects.**

Example #1:

Skating was one of his favorite activities.

In this sentence, the word *"skating"* comes from the verb "skate."

To be sure it is a verbal and not a working verb, we conduct our test:

- We try to apply pronouns to it:

I skating was one of his favorite activities…, you skating was one …, he skating was one…

This doesn't work.

- We also try to change the tense:

Skate was one of... (present tense), *Will skate was one ...* (future tense)

As you can see, such tense changes don't work either. *"Skating"* is not a working verb in the sentence.

Since it has an "-ing" ending, we know it is a <u>gerund</u>. Here it serves as a noun since it represents a happening and is meant to stand alone as the subject of the sentence.

Example #2:

Gliding across the ice, the boy felt graceful.

In this sentence, the word *"gliding"* comes from the verb "glide."

To be sure it is a verbal and not a working verb, we apply our test:

- We apply pronouns to it.

I gliding across the ice, the boy..., *You gliding across the ice...,* *He gliding across the ice...*

- We try to change the tense:

Glide across the ice, the boy... (present tense), *Will glide across the ice...* (future tense)

As you can see, the verbal passes neither part of the test. *"Gliding"* is not a working verb in the sentence.

Since it has an "-ing" ending, we know it is a <u>gerund</u> and, therefore, either a noun or an adjective. Since it modifies (describes) the boy in this sentence, it must be an adjective.

Note: When you find an "-ing" verbal that is preceded by a form of the verb "*to be,*" check to see if the verbal could be changed to the simple present tense (without the verb "*to be*") without changing the intent of the sentence. If it can be, then the verbal plus the verb "*to be*" are the working verb in the progressive form (a form that allows us to write about actions in progress).

Example:

The boy is eating the ice cream.

In this sentence, *"eating"* looks like an "-ing" verbal. However, the verb form "*is*" that precedes it tells us that it might actually be the working verb in the progressive form. To test this theory, we change the verbal to the simple present without "*is*" to see if the writer's intent remains the same:

The boy eats the ice cream.

This action seems to be what the writer was trying to express. Therefore, the working verb of the sentence is *"is eating."*

On the other hand, in the following sentence, the "-ing" word is simply a verbal:

The song is inspiring.

Although a change to simple present still seems to make sense – *"The song inspires"* – the fact that no object has been included in the sentence (inspires what? inspires whom?) tells us that the writer's intent was simply to describe the song. Therefore, the working verb in the sentence is simply *"is." "Inspiring"* is a <u>gerund</u> that works as an adjective. (We'll look at the "progressive form" in more detail later in the text.)

Participles

Participles are verb forms that end in "-ed."

- **Participles are <u>never</u> used as nouns and <u>cannot</u> function as subjects or objects.**
- **Participles <u>cannot</u> create objects.**

Example:

Exhausted, he sat down for a while.

In this sentence, the word *"exhausted"* comes from the verb *"exhaust."* To determine if it is part of a working verb, we apply our test:

- *I exhausted, he sat down..., You exhausted, he sat down..., He exhausted, he sat down...*

This doesn't work. Let's see if it passes the second part of the test.

- *Exhaust, he sat down for a while...* (present tense), *Will exhaust, he sat down ...* (future tense)

As you can see, the tense change definitely doesn't work. Since a working verb must clearly pass both parts of the test, we can conclude that this word is not a working verb in the sentence. It is definitely a participle, and it is, therefore, simply an adjective.

Note: When you find an "-ed" verbal that is preceded by a form of the verb "*to be,*" check to see if you could invert the sentence, attribute the action to an unnamed "someone" or "something," and change the verbal to the simple tense (without the verb "*to be*") without changing the intent of the sentence. If so, then the verbal plus the verb "*to be*" are the working verb in the passive voice (a form that allows us to focus the sentence on the receiver of the action instead of the doer of the action).

Example:

The boy was eliminated from the contest.

The sentence could be inverted and the verb tense could be changed to a simple tense without the verb "*to be*" and still reflect the intended meaning of the message:

[Someone] *eliminated the boy from the contest.*

Even though the doer of the action is not identified in the original sentence, the writer's intent appears to be to describe what happened to the boy, not to describe the state of being the boy found himself in. That means that "*was eliminated*" is the working verb in the passive voice. (We'll discuss "voice" in more detail later in this text.)

Infinitives

Infinitives are verb forms that are usually preceded by the word "to."

- **Infinitives used as nouns can serve as subjects or objects.**
- **Infinitives can create objects.**

Example:

He loves to skate every day.

In this sentence, *"to skate"* is recognizable as a possible verb, so let's test it:

- *He loves to I skate..., He loves to he skates*

- *He loves to skated...* (past tense), *He loves to will skate...* (future tense)

We see that this is obviously not a working verb in the sentence. The word "*to*" in front of it marks it as an infinitive, though sometimes *"to"* is suppressed. Infinitives can serve as nouns, and we see that it is, in fact, the object of the verb *"loves"*: He loves what? He loves to skate.

Prepositions

Prepositions are small words that are used with other words in phrases to indicate the position or relationship of those other words to something within the sentence. They often help us to see how or where something is positioned.

- **Prepositions cannot function as subjects or objects.**
- **Prepositions <u>can</u> create objects.**

Example:

The book was found <u>on</u> the table.

In this sentence, the word *"on"* is a preposition and its object is *"table"* (on what? on the table). The preposition allows us to see the relationship of book to table. The phrase *"on the table"* is called a prepositional phrase because it begins with a preposition. Please refer to Appendix A for a list of prepositions.

Modifiers

<u>Articles</u>

Articles ("the," "a," and "an") are words that modify nouns only.

- **Articles cannot serve as subjects or objects.**
- **Articles cannot create objects.**

Example:

<u>The</u> table you see there is <u>a</u> good example of <u>the</u> furniture style known as Queen Anne.

<u>Adjectives</u>

Adjectives are words that modify (that is, in some way describe or help us to visualize) nouns and pronouns. They represent qualities or characteristics of people, places, things, or ideas, or answer questions such as "what kind?" and "how many?" in relation to those items.

- **Adjectives cannot serve as subjects or objects.**
- **Adjectives cannot create objects.**

Example:

The expensive red vase crashed to the floor and broke into four large pieces.

In this sentence, the underlined words are adjectives that represent qualities or characteristics (*red, large*) or answer the questions "what kind?" (*expensive*) and "how many?" (*four*).

Adverbs

Adverbs are also modifiers, but they only describe verbs, adjectives, or other adverbs. They often end in "-ly."

- **Adverbs cannot serve as subjects or objects.**
- **Adverbs cannot create objects.**

Example:

The man responded too quickly when asked what he had been doing that night.

In this sentence, *"quickly"* is an adverb that modifies the verb *"responded"* (how did he respond? he responded quickly). Notice that *"too"* is also an adverb since it modifies the adverb *"quickly"* (how quickly? too quickly).

Note: You can always tell whether an adjective or an adverb is called for by looking at the type of word being modified.

Conjunctions

Conjunctions are words that help to connect words, phrases, or clauses (i.e., they create "junctions").

There are two major types of conjunctions: coordinating conjunctions and subordinating conjunctions.

Coordinating conjunctions (and, or, nor, for, so, but, yet)

- Coordinating conjunctions are used to link items that are parallel to each other.
- Coordinating conjunctions do not affect the nature of the words they connect to each other. For example, they cannot turn an independent clause into a dependent clause.
- **Coordinating conjunctions cannot function as subjects or objects.**
- **Coordinating conjunctions cannot create objects.**

Coordinating conjunctions can link:

- one word to another word

The pencil and paper...

- one subject to another subject

Tom and Harry joined Dick for lunch.

- one verb to another verb

Jane ate quickly <u>and</u> left for work.

- one object to another object

He wasn't sure whether he should eat the cookie <u>or</u> the slice of pie.

- one adjective to another adjective

The dress was simple <u>yet</u> elegant.

- one phrase to another phrase

Over the hill <u>and</u> through the woods, to their uncle's house they went.

- one dependent clause to another dependent clause

He knew that he was being careless <u>and</u> that he might hurt someone.

- one independent clause to another independent clause.

He was extremely tired, <u>but</u> he kept on driving just the same.

Note: A coordinating conjunction resembles the middle link in a chain. As such, it is meant to connect two parallel or similar items, one at each end. Therefore, this type of conjunction should not normally be used at the beginning of a sentence since, in that position, it dangles like an open link with nothing to hook on to. Although you may occasionally break this "rule" for effect, you always risk weakening your sentence in doing so by making it seem incomplete and by denying your subject the full emphasis it deserves by pushing it out of its rightful spot at the beginning of the sentence. If a connection is needed, look instead for an appropriate transitional word or term, or consider making the idea part of the previous sentence.

Example:

The woman left the room. But her presence was felt through the rest of the meeting.

Possible revisions:

- *The woman left the room. However, her presence was felt through the rest of the meeting.*

or

- *Although the woman left the room, her presence was felt through the rest of the meeting.*

Subordinating conjunctions (words like "because," "although," and "if")

- Subordinating conjunctions are used to link two clauses together and to establish a relationship between one clause and the other (see list in Appendix A). They often help us to determine the "why" or "when" of things.
- Subordinating conjunctions do affect the nature of the clauses they connect by turning one of them into a dependent clause.
- **Subordinating conjunctions cannot function as subjects or objects.**
- **Subordinating conjunctions cannot create objects.**

Example:

I wrote to you <u>because</u> I need help.

If these two clauses were expressed as separate independent thoughts, the causal relationship between them would not be clearly expressed but would remain, at best, merely implied:

I wrote to you, and I need help.

I wrote to you. I need help.

Subordinating conjunctions allow us to control the focus of our message in order to convey ideas in the most meaningful way.

Word Functions

In defining the parts of speech, I've pointed out which ones can or cannot serve as subjects and objects and which ones can or cannot be object-creators. To summarize this information, the following types of words can serve as:

<u>Subjects</u>

- nouns,
- pronouns, and
- gerunds and infinitives working as nouns

<u>Objects</u>

- nouns,
- pronouns, and
- gerunds and infinitives working as nouns

Object-creators

- verbs,
- verbals, and
- prepositions

You've now taken a giant step toward mastering "clause and effect" since you know three very important things about subjects and objects:

- Nouns, pronouns, and words that function as nouns are the only types of words that can function as subjects.
- Nouns, pronouns, and words that function as nouns are the only types of words that can function as objects.
- Verbs, verbals, and prepositions are the only types of words that can create objects.

[Note: Phrases and clauses can sometimes function as nouns and can, therefore, be subjects or objects within a sentence. However, for clarity in explaining the subject/verb identification process that follows, I have focused on nouns instead of noun phrases or noun clauses. One you've mastered the process, these phrases and clauses should cause you very few problems.]

Let's add two more crucial pieces of information to your growing knowledge about language:

- Words that function as nouns and pronouns can perform only one job within any given sentence – that is, they can function either as subjects or as objects, but not as both – and

- Words that function as nouns and pronouns <u>must</u> function as subjects or objects – that is, they cannot remain unemployed .

You are now equipped to learn how to recognize all the subjects and objects in the sentences you read or write, the first and most important step in being able to identify clauses. Please keep these functions in mind as you proceed to the key element of this text: The Subject/Verb Identification Process.

The next chapter embodies my challenge to you:

- Take the time to go through the process, no matter how elementary it may seem to you.
- Read each example in each step carefully until you think you understand the process.
- Go back over the text we've already covered if you need to refresh your memory about parts of speech or about the functions of words.
- Be sure not to skip steps.

Once you've read and understood the 4 steps of the process, pull out a pen and paper and edit the six sample sentences provided at the end of the process. [You'll find suggested edits in the following chapter, but don't look until you're satisfied with your own effort.]

Finally, look at anything you've written recently, or at anything anyone else has written, and see if you can spot the subject/verb combinations more easily as a result of the "object elimination" mechanism you've learned.

- If you can, you're ready to take full advantage of the power of "clause and effect" explained in the later chapters.
- If not, you may want to review the first chapters of this text and try the process again.

Good luck!

PART III: THE SUBJECT/VERB IDENTIFICATION PROCESS

To improve your editing skills by tapping into the benefits of "clause and effect," it's imperative that you be able to spot clauses. Since the key element of a clause is the subject/verb combination around which the clause is built, you have to be able to identify all subjects and verbs in your sentences. The best way to do that is to begin by identifying all the subjects, and the process that follows is designed to help you do just that.

Perhaps you already know how to spot most subjects in the sentences you read or write, but for your editing to improve, "most" is not good enough. You must be able to eliminate non-subjects at a glance, and, unfortunately, what you learned in school has probably not prepared you to do that.

In grammar texts and classes, the standard advice given for finding subjects is: "Find the verb and ask 'who' or 'what' in front of it. Your answer is the subject."

There are two problems with this advice:

- Some writers can't find all the verbs in their sentences, and
- Some writers answer the question in the wrong way.

The first problem, of course, is related to the complexity of the sentences we create and to the existence of words that look like verbs but don't function as verbs in our sentences.

This problem can be overcome once you learn how to recognize verbs and understand the difference between working verbs and verbals. (If the difference between verbs and verbals is still not clear to you, you may want to reread the previous chapter before proceeding.)

The second problem, however, is more difficult to deal with because it stems from the faulty assumption that an action will necessarily lead us to the person or thing that performed the action. In reality, the relationship between the subject and the verb does not stem from the verb. On the contrary, it is the subject that naturally leads us to the action.

Fortunately, there is a better way to identify subjects. The solution rests on your understanding of the following:

- Nouns, pronouns, and words that function as nouns can and must perform one of two possible jobs at any given time within a sentence: they can and must be either subjects or objects.   AND
- These types of words can neither remain unemployed nor perform both functions at once.

If you understand this, you can find your subjects by a process of object-elimination that may seem complex at first but that, after only a few exercises, quickly becomes easy and is remarkably complete and accurate.

Object Elimination

This is where your recognition of object-creators comes into play.

If you recall, there are three types of words that create objects: verbs, verbals, and prepositions. With this knowledge, you can solve the problem of subject identification by first determining whether or not your nouns or pronouns are objects, since it is easier to find objects than subjects. The simple elimination of objects will then leave you with nouns or pronouns that must function as subjects. This process of elimination is complete and accurate because it takes into account every potential subject in even the most complex sentence.

This process works more easily and more accurately than the traditional subject identification method because of the following factors:

- Objects are easier to find than subjects because they normally appear in the sentence after the words that create them. More versatile are subjects since they sometimes appear after their verbs and are harder to locate (as the first clause in this sentence demonstrates).
- You will normally search for an object-creator in a more limited and clearly defined space than you might search for a subject.
- It's usually easier to identify an object (direct or indirect) correctly by asking "whom," "what," or, in some cases, "when" or "where" after the object-creator because the relationship between the creator and its object stems from the creator. The relationship between a subject and a verb, on the other hand, does not stem from the verb, so asking "who" or "what" before the verb can be misleading.

The first few times you apply this process, you should take the time to analyze each and every noun and pronoun in your sentences. You'll find that, once you've analyzed even just a half dozen sentences, your ability to spot objects will have increased dramatically. Before long, you should be able to identify all the subjects in even the most complex sentences almost at a glance. Once you know where your subjects are, you can then ask: what is the subject doing or being? This will lead you to the working verbs, and you'll thus be armed with the skill of locating clauses (subject/verb combinations) – the real key to improving your writing.

NOTE: If you want to benefit from this book, please don't skip this process. If the word "process" scares you, or if you are intimidated by directions, remind yourself of the successes you've experienced all your life in learning new ways of doing things. Something as basic as tying a shoelace, for example, is a surprisingly complicated skill that you mastered as a child. (If you don't believe it's a complicated skill, try writing directions for it.) You now perform that skill automatically without even thinking about how you do it. This is what I would like you to keep in mind as you approach the process that follows. Though it may seem complicated at first glance, it's less complicated than tying a shoelace, and you're not a small child trying to master it.

Mastering this process is key to improving your writing and editing skills no matter how skillful you already are. I can almost guarantee that, if you read the directions attentively and do the recommended exercises (these involve only a half-dozen sample sentences), you'll begin to acquire that "automatic" ability to analyze sentence structure that is essential to editing. Furthermore, everything else in this book will fall into place.

Here goes...

THE SUBJECT/VERB IDENTIFICATION PROCESS

The purpose of this process is to allow you to locate all the **clauses** – i.e., the subject/verb combinations – in the sentences you read and write in order to be able to benefit from "Clause and Effect." Simply follow the steps in sequence, even if you think you can already spot clauses without difficulty. If you bother to go through the process a couple of times, the effort should alter the way you look at sentences, making it easier for you to spot true subject/verb combinations just by scanning what you read.

STEP 1

Scan the entire sentence you want to edit to locate all the words that look like relative or demonstrative pronouns (*this, that, who, which*, or related forms of these words).

- If you find no relative or demonstrative pronouns in your sentence, go on to step 2.
- If you do find a relative or demonstrative pronoun and it is followed immediately by a verb, underline the pronoun as a potential subject.
- If the relative or demonstrative pronoun is followed immediately by a noun or pronoun, strike it out.

(Exception: If the noun or pronoun is part of an editorial clause such as "I feel" or "you thought" and that clause is followed by a working verb, underline the relative or demonstrative pronoun as a potential subject. Example: "This sentence, which I feel provides you with a good example of the concept I'm trying to explain, should be helpful to you." As you can see, I've underlined "which" because the clause "I feel" is followed immediately by the verb "provides.")

Example 1:

The police officer who had just spoken to us tagged the car that was parked in that "No Parking" zone.

We begin by scanning this sentence to see if there are any relative and/or demonstrative pronouns. We find that *"who"* and the first *that* are subjects since they are followed immediately by verbs (*had spoken* & *was*). I've underlined these words to indicate that they are definitely subjects.

The second *"that"* is followed immediately by a noun and its modifier *("No Parking" zone)*, so I've crossed it out.

Example 2:

I lost the letter that you sent me last week.

In this sentence, we can assume that the pronoun *"that"* is not a subject since it is followed immediately by a pronoun (*you*), so I've crossed it out.

Example 3:

~~That~~ *coat is not mine.*

In this sentence, *"that"* is followed by a noun (*coat*), so I've crossed it out.

Example 4:

Of all the problems he encountered, <u>this</u> was definitely the worst one.

In this sentence, which actually means *"Of all the problems* [that] *he encountered…,"* the relative pronoun *"that"* would be crossed out since it is followed by a pronoun. The demonstrative pronoun *"this"* is followed by a verb (*was*), so it is underlined.

Example 5:

The extremely tired circus troupe made mistakes throughout the performance.

There are no relative pronouns, so we need do nothing in this step.

Example 6:

He cried and pouted when I said "No!" because he really wanted to eat the cookie.

There are no relative pronouns, so we need do nothing in this step.

Example 7:

I understand you are leaving us soon.

Although there is a relative pronoun in this sentence (*that*), it is not stated, so we need do nothing in this step. It would be crossed out since it is followed by a pronoun.

STEP 2

Next, go back to the beginning of the sentence and locate the first noun or personal pronoun in the sentence.

- Examine the words that precede that noun or pronoun. In other words, scan the sentence backwards from the first noun or pronoun back to the beginning of the sentence.
- If no object-creators (i.e., verbs, verbals, or prepositions) precede the first noun or personal pronoun you've identified, underline it and go on to Step 3.
- If there are object-creators in front of the first noun or personal pronoun, cross it out and search for the next noun or personal pronoun in the sentence. Keep doing this until you've found the first noun or personal pronoun you can underline, and go on to Step 3.

As you carry out Step 2, please note the following:

- "*There*" can never be a subject or an object, so cross it out if you find it and look for the next noun or pronoun.
- A noun that is followed immediately by another noun is usually working as an adjective. Cross it out because adjectives can never be subjects, and focus on the second noun.

Example 1:

The ~~police~~ <u>officer</u> <u>who</u> had just spoken to us tagged the car <u>that</u> was parked in ~~that~~ "No Parking" zone.

In this sentence in which we've already identified *"who"* and *"that"* as potential subjects using Step 1, the first noun we encounter is *"police,"* but we notice that it is followed immediately by a second noun (*officer*), so we cross it out because it is serving as an adjective and cannot be a subject. Instead, we focus on *"officer"* as the first noun in the sentence. When we scan backwards to determine what kinds of words come before it, we reach the beginning capital without finding an object-creator, so I've underlined it as a subject.

Example 2:

<u>I</u> lost the letter ~~that~~ you sent me last week.

In this sentence, the first noun or personal pronoun is "I". Since nothing precedes it, we can assume that it is a subject, so I've underlined it.

Example 3:

~~That~~ <u>coat</u> is not mine.

In this sentence, *"coat"* is the first noun we encounter. Since it has no object-creator in front of it, I've underlined it as a subject.

Example 4:

Of all the ~~*problems*~~ *[~~that~~]* <u>*he*</u> *encountered,* <u>*this*</u> *was definitely the worst one.*

In this sentence, the first noun (*problems*) is preceded by an object-creator – the preposition *"of"* – and is the object of that preposition (of what? of all the problems), so I've crossed it out as a potential subject. (In this sentence, by the way, *"all"* serves as an adjective that answers the question "how many" – how many problems? all the problems.) The next potential subject I see is the pronoun *"he."* It is not the object of the preposition, nor is it preceded by any other object-creator, so I've underlined it as the first subject.

Example 5:

The extremely tired ~~*circus*~~ <u>*troupe*</u> *made mistakes throughout the performance.*

In this sentence, the first noun (*circus*) is immediately followed by another noun (*troupe*), so I've crossed out circus because it serves as a modifier. Since no object-creators precede *"troupe,"* I've underlined it as a subject.

Example 6:

<u>*He*</u> *cried and pouted when I said "No!" because he really wanted to eat the cookie.*

The first noun or personal pronoun is *"he."* Since nothing precedes it, I've underlined it as a subject.

Example 7:

I understand [~~that~~] *you are leaving us soon.*

The first noun or personal pronoun is "*I*". Since nothing precedes it, I've underlined it as a subject.

STEP 3

Find the next noun or personal pronoun in each sentence and apply to it the process described in Step 2. Do this for all the remaining nouns and pronouns in the sentence.

As you scan backwards from each noun or pronoun, if you reach an object-creator – i.e., a verb, verbal, or preposition – ask "whom" or "what" (or "when," "where," or "to whom" to find indirect objects of verbs) after that word.

- If your answer is the single noun or pronoun whose function you are trying to identify, that noun or pronoun is an object, so cross it out.
- If the answer to the question you ask after an object-creator is a group of words of which the noun or pronoun is a part, then the single noun or pronoun is not an object and must be a subject. Underline it. (For example, in the sentence "*It took a while before he discovered you were gone*," "*you*" is preceded by an object-creator – the verb "*discovered*" – but is not the object of that verb. What "*he discovered*" is not "*you*" but "[that] *you were gone.*" Had the relative pronoun "*that*" not been suppressed, it would have served as a barrier that would have made it evident that "*you*" must be a subject.)

- If you reach any one of the barriers listed below before coming across an object-creator, stop your search and assume that your noun or pronoun is a subject. Underline the word and move on to the next noun or pronoun.

List of barriers:

- A subordinating conjunction (refer to list in Appendix A).
- A relative pronoun that you've already crossed out.
- The capital letter that marks the beginning of the sentence you're analyzing.
- A period or semi-colon or any sentence-ending punctuation. [Note: Don't consider a semi-colon used to separate items in a list to be a barrier.]

Remember: Articles (*a*, *an*, *the*), coordinating conjunctions, and modifiers (words working as adjectives or adverbs) are not object- creators, so ignore them as you scan your sentences.

Example 1:

The ~~police~~ officer who had just spoken to ~~us~~ tagged the ~~car~~ that was parked ~~in that~~ "~~No Parking~~" ~~zone~~.

In this sentence, in which we've already identified three subjects, the next noun or pronoun (*us*) is preceded by the preposition "*to*." Since it is the object of the preposition (we ask "to whom?" and get the answer "to us"), I've crossed it out.

The next noun (*car*) is preceded by the verb *"tagged."* If we ask "tagged what?", we discover that the officer tagged the *"car." "Car"* is, therefore, the object of the verb *"tagged."* Since it is an object, it cannot function as a subject, so I've crossed it out.

The final noun (*zone*) is object of the preposition *"in"* that precedes it (in what? in the zone). Note that *"No Parking"* is an adjective phrase since it describes *"zone."* Since none of these words can function as subjects, I've crossed them all out.

Example 2:

<u>I</u> lost the ~~letter~~ ~~that~~ <u>you</u> sent ~~me~~ last ~~week~~.

In this sentence, the next noun is *"letter."* It is the object of the verb that precedes it (we ask *"lost what?"* and get the answer *"lost the letter),* so I've crossed it out.

The pronoun *"you"* is preceded by a barrier – in this case, a relative pronoun that we've already crossed out – so I've underlined it as a subject.

The next pronoun (*me*) is preceded by the preposition *"to,"* which is not stated but is "understood" to be functioning in the sentence, and is the object of that preposition (we ask *"sent [to] whom?"* and we get the answer *"sent [to] me"*). Because it can't be a subject, I've crossed it out.

The final noun (*week*) is the indirect object of the verb that precedes it (we ask "sent when?" and we get the answer "sent last week"). Because it can't be a subject, I've crossed it out.

Example 3:

~~That~~ <u>coat</u> is not ~~mine~~.

In this sentence, the only noun or pronoun other than "*coat*" is the possessive pronoun "*mine,*" which in this sentence is the predicate of the verb "*is*" which precedes it. Since the verb "*to be*" serves as an equals sign, the predicate is considered to be in the subjective case since it is equal to the subject (*coat* = *mine*, which really means "my coat"). However, since we usually identify the first term in such an equation as the true subject of the sentence, for this exercise I've crossed out the predicate.

Example 4:

Of ~~all~~ the ~~problems~~ [~~that~~] <u>he</u> encountered, <u>this</u> was definitely the worst ~~one~~.

In this sentence, the only other potential subject in this sentence is the pronoun "*one,*" which is preceded by the verb "*was,*" a form of the verb "*to be.*" As such, it is a predicate in the subjective case but is not, for our purposes, a subject, so I've crossed it out.

Example 5:

The extremely tired circus <u>troupe</u> *made* ~~mistakes~~ *throughout the* ~~performance~~.

In this sentence, the noun *"mistakes"* is preceded by a verb (*made*) and is the direct object of that verb (made what? made mistakes), so I've crossed it out. The noun *"performance"* is preceded by a preposition (*throughout*) and is the object of that preposition (throughout what? throughout the performance), so I've crossed it out as well. There are no other pronouns or nouns in this sentence.

Example 6:

<u>He</u> *cried and pouted when* <u>I</u> *said "*~~No~~*!" because* <u>he</u> *really wanted to eat the* ~~cookie~~.

In this sentence, the personal pronoun *"I"* is preceded by the subordinating conjunction *"when,"* one of the barriers listed above. Therefore, I've underlined *"I"* as a subject.

The next word that appears to serve as a noun, *"No,"* is preceded by a verb (*"said"*) and is the object of that verb (said what? said "No!"), so I've crossed it out. The next pronoun (*"he"*) is preceded by the subordinating conjunction *"because,"* so I've underlined it.

The last noun, *"cookie,"* is preceded by the infinitive *"to eat"* and is the object of that verbal (to eat what? to eat the cookie), so I've crossed it out.

Example 7:

I understand [~~that~~] *you are leaving ~~us~~ soon.*

In this sentence, the pronoun *"you"* is preceded by a barrier – a relative pronoun that we've already crossed out – so I've underlined it as a subject. [Note: Even if you hadn't recognized that the relative pronoun was understood in this sentence, you'd know that *"you"* is a subject because it is not the object of the verb that appears to precede it. The answer to "understand what?" is not the single word but the entire clause (I understand what? I understand "you are leaving."]

The second pronoun (*us*) is preceded by a verb (*are leaving* – yes, it's a verb in the progressive form). Since the answer to "are leaving whom?" is *"us,"* the pronoun is an object, so I've crossed it out.

STEP 4

Once you've completed the process of identifying all the possible subjects in your sentence, ask what those subjects are doing or being within the sentence and you'll find the working verbs that they are linked to. These subject/verb combinations form the major element of each of your clauses.

Example 1:

The police <u>officer</u> <u>who</u> had just spoken to us tagged the car <u>that</u> was parked in the "No Parking" zone.

If you ask what the subjects are doing in this sentence (e.g., what did the officer do? the officer tagged the car), you'll discover the following:

- The <u>officer</u> <u>tagged</u> the car = clause #1;
- <u>who</u> <u>had</u> just <u>spoken</u> to us = clause #2; and
- <u>that</u> <u>was</u> parked in the "No Parking" zone = clause #3.

Example 2:

I lost the letter that <u>you</u> sent me last week.

In this sentence:

- <u>I</u> <u>lost</u> the letter = clause #1, and
- that <u>you</u> <u>sent</u> me last week = clause #2

Example 3:

That <u>coat</u> is not mine.

In this sentence:

- That <u>coat</u> <u>is</u> not mine = the only clause in the sentence.

Example 4:

Of all the problems [that] <u>he</u> encountered, <u>this</u> was definitely the worst one.

In this sentence:

- Of all the problems [that] <u>he</u> <u>encountered</u> = clause #1, and
- <u>this</u> <u>was</u> definitely the worst one = clause #2.

Example 5:

The extremely tired circus <u>troupe</u> made mistakes throughout the performance.

In this sentence:

- The extremely tired circus <u>troupe</u> <u>made</u> mistakes throughout the performance = the only clause in the sentence.

Example 6:

<u>He</u> cried and pouted when <u>I</u> said "~~No!~~" because <u>he</u> really wanted to eat the ~~cookie~~.

In this sentence:

- <u>He</u> <u>cried</u> and <u>pouted</u> = clause #1,
- when <u>I</u> <u>said</u> "No!" = clause #2, and
- because <u>he</u> really <u>wanted</u> to eat the cookie = clause #3.

Example 7:

<u>I</u> understand [that] <u>you</u> are leaving us soon.

In this sentence:

- <u>I</u> <u>understand</u> = clause #1, and
- [that] <u>you</u> <u>are leaving</u> us soon = clause #2.

Now it's your turn.

I invite you to try your hand at the process. In analyzing the following sentences (and don't worry about the grammatical errors in these sentences), please follow each of the 4 steps in sequence. By the sixth time you apply the process, you should be able to spot subject/verb combinations without effort. When you're done, turn to the next chapter to verify what you've found and to see what you can learn from your discoveries.

SAMPLE SENTENCES

1. *The tremendous response we experienced from our advertisement for the publications have exhausted our supply.*

2. *There was also the Displaced Home Makers that I was involved with.*

3. *The time it takes to put the codes in the computer to sell something is very time-consuming.*

4. *Your advertisement for someone to work in your office is just the kind of experience I need.*

5. *There are some payments made that are never entered into the computer.*

6. *My experience dealing with customers range from handling routine inquiries to resolving difficult collection matters.*

7. *Only one of the books include the reference you're looking for.*

PART IV – THE PAYOFF

The following analysis of the sentences you just tackled should give you some idea of the **effect** an ability to spot **clauses** (i.e., subject/verb combinations) can have on the quality of your editing skills. Subsequent chapters will focus on additional things you should know about clauses and will illustrate the effects that can result from that knowledge.

So let's begin...

1. *The tremendous <u>response</u> <u>we</u> <u>experienced</u> from our advertisement for the publications <u>have exhausted</u> our supply.*

    - Clause #1 – The tremendous <u>response</u> <u>have exhausted</u> our supply
    - Clause #2 – [that] <u>we</u> <u>experienced</u> from our advertisement for the publications

Now that you have spotted the clauses, what effect does this knowledge have on your ability to correct and/or improve the sentence? In other words, what editing choices now present themselves more clearly to you as you look at the written words?

Choice #1

- You could begin by correcting the subject/verb agreement error in clause #1.

The tremendous response has exhausted our supply.

Choice #2

- You could then make the sentence more concise by turning clause #2 – a dependent clause that merely serves to explain one element of the first clause – into a prepositional phrase. This would lead you to correct the preposition error in the sentence.

The tremendous response to our advertisement for the publications has exhausted our supply.

Choice #3

- You could change the focus of the sentence from "the response" to "we" or to "supply," if that better suited your purpose, simply by changing your subjects and determining which of the clauses should be independent and which should be dependent.

We experienced such a tremendous response to our advertisement for the publications that our supply has been exhausted. or

Our supply has been exhausted as a result of the tremendous response to our advertisement for the publications.

2. **There <u>was</u> also the <u>Displaced Home Makers</u> that <u>I was</u> involved with.**

   - Clause #1 – There <u>was</u> also the <u>Displaced Home Makers</u>
   - Clause #2 – that <u>I was</u> involved with.

Notice that the subject of clause #1, the independent clause in this sentence, has been displaced from its key position at the beginning of the sentence by use of the pronoun "*there*," which itself cannot be a subject. The clause has been further weakened because its only purpose is to point to the subject, not to say anything about it.

Choice #1:

- You could strengthen the independent clause simply by putting the real subject in its place and saying something specific about it:

Displaced Home Makers was another worthwhile group that I was involved with.

Choice #2:

- You could use an action verb instead of merely describing a state of being and eliminate the dependent clause entirely.

Displaced Home Makers also welcomed me as a member.

Both options assume that you want to focus on the organization.

Choice #3:

- It is interesting to note, however, that the subject of clause #2, the dependent clause, is the more forceful "*I*". The real message seems to be that "*I*" was involved with a certain organization, so if your intent is to focus on your involvement rather than on the organization, you can state that directly and forcefully in one independent clause.

I was also involved with Displaced Home Makers.

3. **The <u>time</u> <u>it</u> <u>takes</u> to put the codes in the computer to sell something <u>is</u> very time-consuming.**

- Clause #1 – The <u>time</u> <u>is</u> very time-consuming
- Clause #2 – [that] <u>it</u> <u>takes</u> to put the codes in the computer to sell something

Obviously, the writer didn't pay attention to the main idea being conveyed in this sentence. "The time is time-consuming" does not make sense. Notice, too, that the independent clause is merely descriptive and the subject/verb combination in the dependent clause ("*it takes*") says nothing.

What is the real subject? It is the action of putting codes into the computer to sell something.

Choice #1:

- You can focus on the real subject by placing it in the main clause, which allows you to eliminate the dependent clause entirely:

Putting codes into the computer to sell something is very time-consuming.

Choice #2:

- This simplification allows you to see more clearly how you can improve the wording by using a better subject and reducing a whole phrase (*"to sell something"*) to a single adjective.

Entering sales codes into the computer is very time-consuming.

Often, improving one element of a sentence allows you to see other possibilities for improvement. We'll explore some of those possibilities in a later chapter.

4. ***Your <u>advertisement</u> for someone to work in your office <u>is</u> just the kind of experience <u>I need</u>.***

   - Clause #1 – Your <u>advertisement</u> for someone to work in your office <u>is</u> just the kind of experience
   - Clause #2 – [that] <u>I need</u>

In this complex sentence, the independent clause tells us that an advertisement *"is"* a *"kind of experience."* If you remember that the verb *"to be"* works like an equals sign within a sentence, you see immediately that this clause doesn't make sense because an advertisement is not usually considered the equivalent of an experience. The verb is inappropriate.

Choice #1:

- You can find a more appropriate verb for the main clause in order to improve the whole sentence.

Your advertisement for someone to work in your office describes just the kind of experience I need.

Choice #2:

- The second choice you could make relates to the reason for writing the sentence, which appears to be to apply for a job. The dependent clause could make you sound too "needy" in this context. You could, therefore, find a more appropriate verb for the dependent clause.

Your advertisement for someone to work in your office describes just the kind of experience [that] I'm looking for.

Although this sentence could use further reworking, choosing more appropriate verbs makes the message more understandable and should make it easier to find ways to improve it further.

5. **There <u>are</u> some <u>payments</u> <u>made</u> <u>that</u> are never entered into the computer.**

  - Clause #1 – There <u>are</u> some <u>payments</u> <u>made</u>
  - Clause #2 – <u>that</u> <u>are</u> never <u>entered</u> into the computer.

Here again, the main subject has been pushed out of its place by *"there,"* which can never be a subject.

Choice #1:

- You can put the subject in its rightful place.

Some payments are made that are never entered into the computer.

Now that you've straightened out the sentence, you can perhaps see that the main clause says very little since the word "payments" inherently implies that a transaction has been *"made."*

Choice #2:

- You can now focus the sentence on the real message and eliminate the dependent clause:

Some payments are never entered into the computer.

6. **My <u>experience</u> dealing with customers range from handling routine inquiries to resolving difficult collection matters.**

    - Clause — My <u>experience</u> dealing with customers <u>range</u> from handling routine inquiries to resolving collection matters.

In this sentence, the subject of the independent clause (the only clause) is a third-person singular word. On the other hand, the verb ending of "*range*" reflects the third-person plural. (Remember that, with verbs, the singular ending takes an "s" and the plural doesn't.)

Choice:

- You can correct the sentence by making the subject and verb agree.

My experience dealing with customers ranges from handling routine inquiries to resolving difficult collection matters.

7. *Only <u>one</u> of the books include the reference <u>you're</u> looking for.*

- Clause #1 – Only <u>one</u> of the books <u>include</u> the reference
- Clause #2 – [that] <u>you're</u> <u>looking</u> for.

In this sentence, the subject of the independent clause is singular but the verb is plural.

Choice:

- You can correct the sentence by making the subject and verb agree.

Only one of the books includes the reference you're looking for.

Are you ready to move on?

I trust that you are starting to see how valuable understanding "clause and effect" can be. The next chapter will deal with how clauses fit into sentences and how an understanding of clauses can help you make sense of punctuation.

PART V -- PUNCTUATION

If you want to write effectively, you must understand the rules of punctuation. Keeping the sentence space in mind, you know that the reader must be given clues as to how words, phrases, and clauses are meant to fit into and work within that space.

Types of complete sentences

As I mentioned at the beginning of this text, in order to create a complete sentence, you must include at least one complete thought – i.e., at least one independent clause – within your sentence space. You may, of course, include additional independent clauses and one or more dependent clauses within the same space. Specific names are given to various types of complete sentences, depending on the number and type of clauses they contain:

- Simple sentences include only one independent clause and no dependent clauses.
- Compound sentences include more than one independent clause and no dependent clauses.
- Complex sentences include one independent clause and at least one dependent clause.
- Compound/complex sentences include at least two independent clauses and at least one dependent clause.

Knowing these definitions will allow us to discuss style, which has a lot to do with how you use clauses within your sentence spaces.

Emphasis in simple, compound, complex, and compound/complex sentences

Imagine the space your sentence occupies as representing a degree of emphasis equal to 100%. If a single independent clause occupies that space, it assumes 100% of the emphasis available in that space. This is why simple sentences are so forceful.

If two independent clauses are presented within the space, they share that 100% equally – that is, they each assume 50% of the emphasis. This fact should help you to decide when you can afford to group parallel independent ideas within the same sentence space.

If the space contains an independent clause and a dependent clause, then the independent clause might assume 75% of the emphasis, with the dependent clause taking on the remaining 25%. Complex sentences help readers to see the relative importance of ideas that are not parallel in significance.

The percentages would change, of course, as more clauses are stuffed within a given sentence space.

Clauses, sentence structure, and the use of punctuation

The normal order of ideas presented within an American English sentence and expressed as clauses is:

- Independent clause [followed by] *dependent clause* (if any).

Most of your readers will expect to see ideas presented in this order within the sentences they read. When the order is inverted or otherwise disrupted, this fact should become quickly evident to your reader so that the clarity and meaning of your message is not affected. The inversion or disruption is normally signaled through the use of punctuation.

When the clauses are in this normal order within a sentence space, there is usually no need for additional punctuation unless the dependent clause expresses an idea that is contrary or opposite to the one expressed in the independent clause and/or calls for special emphasis.

Example:

I went to the store because I needed some milk.

In this sentence, "*I went to the store*" is the independent clause, and "*because I needed some milk*" is the dependent clause. The sentence is in the normal order and requires no extra punctuation.

Example:

I bought two gallons of milk, even though I needed only one.

In this sentence, "*I bought two gallons of milk*" is the independent clause, and "*even though I needed only one*" is the dependent clause. Although this sentence is in the normal order, a comma may be added between the clauses (though the sentence would be fine without it) to stress the fact that the dependent clause expresses an idea that opposes the one expressed in the independent clause.

Inverted order

When the sentence order is inverted, a comma should separate the dependent clause from the independent one to signal the inversion.

- *Dependent clause*, independent clause.

Example:

Because I needed some milk, I went to the store.

The dependent clause begins this sentence. To allow the reader to determine quickly where the main clause really begins, a comma is used to separate the clauses.

Interrupted order

Sometimes a dependent clause is inserted into the middle of an independent clause. If the dependent clause expresses or is attached to a modifier that expresses an idea that is <u>essential</u> to the reader's understanding of the main clause or of a word in the main clause, then no extra punctuation is called for.

Interrupted order with essential clause:

- Independent *dependent clause* clause.

Let's turn to the original sample sentence we used at the beginning of this text:

The car that was towed out of the parking lot belonged to Paul.

In this sentence, "*that was towed out of the parking lot*" is a dependent clause that has been inserted into the main clause. No extra punctuation has been added to this sentence because the dependent clause is essential to our understanding of which car the writer is referring to.

On the other hand, if the dependent clause expresses an idea that is <u>not essential</u> to the reader's understanding of the main clause or of a particular word within the main clause, it should be surrounded by commas.

Interrupted order with non-essential clause:

- Independent, *dependent clause*, clause.

Example:

Paul's car, which didn't start this morning, was towed out of the parking lot.

In this sentence, the dependent clause "*which didn't start this morning*" is surrounded by commas because it is <u>not essential</u> to our understanding of the main clause or of which car the writer is referring to. The punctuation allows the reader to identify information that could be lifted from the text without destroying the meaning.

Compound sentences

In compound sentences, of course, two or more independent clauses follow each other. Failure to properly punctuate independent clauses within a sentence space leads to what is referred to as a "run-on" error.

Remember that independent clauses are meant to stand on their own. Unlike dependent clauses, they are self-sufficient. Therefore, if they are not properly separated from each other by a comma AND a coordinating conjunction, or by a semicolon, they run into each other – hence the term "run-on." The result can be distracting to the reader and can muddle the meaning of your message.

Proper punctuation of compound sentences includes the following choices:

- Independent clause, *coordinating conjunction* independent clause.

Example:

The car was towed, and Paul had to pay a fine to retrieve it.

- Independent clause; independent clause.

Example:

Paul was not happy; he found it hard not to lash out at the officer.

Your choice will depend on the degree of separation you want to establish between the two complete thoughts. Of course, you also have the choice of giving each independent clause its own sentence space or of subordinating one of the clauses to show the relationship between the ideas being expressed.

Compound-complex sentences

In compound-complex sentences, you must determine which independent clauses the dependent clauses are attached to and then punctuate accordingly. There are many possibilities, among them the following:

- Independent clause *dependent clause*; *dependent clause*, independent clause.

Example:

He went home as soon as he could; though he had left the office early, he was now late for dinner.

Notice that the first set of clauses (independent + dependent) is in the normal order and requires no separating punctuation, whereas the second set (dependent + independent) is in the inverted order and requires the comma. The two sets of clauses, which each represent complete thoughts, are then separated by a semi-colon to prevent a run-on error.

- *Dependent clause,* independent clause, *coordinating conjunction* independent clause *dependent clause*.

Example:

When she heard the story, his wife reacted sympathetically, and he was able to relax sooner than he had hoped.

Notice that the first set of clauses (dependent + independent) is in inverted order and requires a comma; the second set (independent + dependent) is in the normal order and requires no additional punctuation; and the two sets require a separator (in this case, a comma and a coordinating conjunction) to prevent a run-on error.

As you can see, being able to recognize clauses will make it easier for you to punctuate your sentences.

What you'll want to remember is that, any time the normal order of a sentence is disturbed, the reader is taken by surprise. Therefore, if you disturb the normal structure of a sentence, be sure:

- You have a reason for doing so, and
- You've given your readers the punctuation clues that will enable them to read and understand your message without difficulty.

Now let's look more closely at the punctuation marks that are most commonly used to control the flow of words in a sentence.

The period (.)

This mark is used to end sentences. As you've already learned, it is one of the indicators of the existence of a sentence space.

Example:

History is an interesting subject.

The comma (,)

This mark is used to separate items such as words, phrases, and clauses.

- When used in pairs, it encloses an item to set it off from the regular text and make clear to the reader that the item is not placed where it would normally be found or is a non-essential yet intended part of the message.
- When used as a single mark or as part of a series of marks, it is meant to be a barrier to indicate an intended break between items.

Although the comma is the weakest of the punctuation marks in terms of interrupting the flow of ideas, its inappropriate use can distort or destroy your message.

There are basically seven reasons why you would use commas:

- Reason #1: To set off an introductory word or phrase at the beginning of a sentence

Single words or phrases that begin sentences but are not part of the main subject are normally set off by a comma to alert the reader to their status as non-subjects since readers will normally expect to find the main subject at the head of the sentence.

Example:

Tired, he went to bed early. ("*Tired*" is a verbal that modifies the subject.)

First of all, I'd like to introduce the participants. ("*First of all*" is a transitional phrase.)

With so much going for him, the boy was bound to succeed in life. ("*With so much going for him*" is a phrase that modifies the subject.)

- Reason #2: To enclose transitions, non-essential words, phrases, or clauses, or words set in apposition within a sentence

Single words, phrases, or even clauses that interrupt the idea being expressed within the sentence space to insert a description, a transition, or an editorial comment are usually enclosed within a pair of commas.

Examples:

The president, however, is doing his best.

The house, thank God, was spared during the recent fire.

That rumor, I'd be willing to bet, is completely false.

My neighbor, a real friend, mowed my lawn while I was away.

- Reason #3: Before a coordinating conjunction to separate two independent clauses within a sentence in order to prevent a run-on error

Two independent clauses within a sentence space are often linked by a comma and a coordinating conjunction.

Example:

The audience roared, and the team regained its momentum.

- Reason #4: To separate items in a list

Lists of nouns, adjectives, verbs, adverbs, phrases, or even clauses are usually separated by commas; semicolons can be used if the items in the list require commas of their own.

Example:

The dog ate the bone, the biscuit, the donut, and the T-bone steak.

The meeting was attended by Mr. Jones, the President; Ms. Smith, the Vice-President; Ms. Readfield, the Secretary; and Mr. Williams, the Consultant.

The nervous man smiled, then cried, and eventually made a complete fool of himself.

As a result of the powerful wind storm, the window broke, the roof tiles flew off, and the telephone wires snapped.

Note: Although the last comma before the "*and*" is optional, it's usually best to use it to keep the list clear and parallel.

- Reason #5: To separate a word, phrase, or dependent clause from the independent clause that precedes it when emphasis is needed to stress contrast between the separated items

Example:

The play was interesting, although the acting was mediocre.

- Reason #6: To separate dependent clauses from independent clauses when the natural order of clauses has been inverted

Example:

Because he overslept, he missed a very important meeting.

- Reason #7: To help clarify potentially ambiguous phrasings – for example, when the reader might mistake which terms are linked by "*and*" when more than one "*and*" is used in a sentence

Example:

The books explain how teachers teach and how children learn, and give examples to illustrate the basic principles of each process.

In this sentence, the comma after "*learn*" is used to be sure that the reader recognizes that the second "*and*" links "*give*" to "*explain*" and not to "*learn.*"

Some professional fiction writers who indulge in page-long sentences have been known to use commas before verbs to help the reader identify extraordinarily long and involved subjects; however, for your reader's sake, you'd do well to keep your sentences reasonable in length and forego this particular use of the comma. (As a rule, commas should NEVER be used for the express purpose of separating a subject from its verb or a verb from its object.)

Note: Nowhere in the list of reasons to use commas do you find the following reason: "To allow the reader to pause for breath." We'd be in real trouble if this were a legitimate reason to punctuate with commas since some readers pause after every other word.

The semicolon (;)

This mark is stronger than a comma and weaker than a period.

There are two major reasons why you would use a semicolon:

- Reason #1: To separate independent clauses when no comma and coordinating conjunction is used between them

Example:

The boy ate the cookie; the girl drank the milk.

- Reason #2: To separate items in a list when commas are used within the items themselves

Example:

I visited Ray, whose home is near mine; John, who lives a half-mile away; and Susan, who lives in the next town.

Note: NEVER use a semicolon to set off a single word, phrase, or dependent clause by itself.

The colon (:)

This mark is used to point the reader to the information that follows it.

- It can be used as end punctuation that is followed by text that begins with a capital letter, or
- It can be viewed as a gateway within the sentence and followed by lower case text that completes the sentence.

The choice you make depends on how much of a break you intend to create between the material that comes before the mark and the words that follow it.

Example:

There are two vegetables I really dislike: broccoli and cooked celery.

I've come up with a really great idea: Let's have a family reunion!

The dash (–)

This mark is used to physically separate a word, phrase, or clause from the rest of the text for emphasis or clarity.

It should be used sparingly because, although it can create emphasis, it also disrupts the normal flow of ideas and visually distracts the reader.

Example:

The three guys mentioned in the article – Bob, Joe, and Ted – are super athletes.

Unfortunately, the dash is often used as a substitute for correct punctuation.

Parentheses ( )

This pair of marks is used to enclose information that is not part of the basic message but has been added as a supplement or as an aside to the reader.

This form of punctuation, which distracts the reader from the main message, should be used sparingly, though its judicious use can be an effective way of creating emphasis.

Example:

The new law reflects a real lack of common sense (which comes as a surprise, I'm sure) on the part of the legislators.

The question mark (?)

This mark is meant to be used as end punctuation and indicates that a question is being asked. Without it, the reader has no way of detecting the nature of the idea being presented.

Example:

What do you mean by that?

The exclamation point (!)

This mark is also meant to be used as end punctuation.

* It is used to emphasize the words or ideas expressed or to indicate surprise or astonishment.

Be careful not to overuse it because it becomes surprisingly weak after its initial use.

Example:

He actually told me he loved me!

Quotation marks (" ")

These marks are used to indicate quoted material or to enclose special words or terms.

The reader should recognize immediately why they've been used; otherwise, they are useless.

When you use quotation marks, remember:

* Commas and periods are usually placed within the quotes; other ending punctuation (exclamation points, question marks) are placed (a) within the quotes if they apply to the quoted material, or (b) outside the quotes if they apply to the main clause of the sentence.
* End-of-sentence punctuation is never used twice in the same sentence. (Refer to more detailed grammar texts for further information.)

Example:

When I heard him say "I love you," I nearly fell over. Then he turned to me and asked, "Are you surprised?" Do you think he believed me when I simply said "Not at all"?

Word of caution about punctuation

Remember that anything that unnecessarily distracts the reader and interrupts the flow of ideas weakens your message. Furthermore, incorrect punctuation can, in some instances, change the meaning of your message, sometimes with dire consequences.

Punctuation Challenge

Here are some sentences if you'd like to test what you've just learned. You'll find them punctuated properly in Appendix C.

- *Spring is the most exciting season of the year for me, because I think of it as a time of renewal.*

- *I like riding through the White Mountains, to see the view, it's simply breathtaking.*

- *We pack everything in the pick-up and drive to every brook we can find.*

- *I can't ice skate but I sometimes go with my girlfriend because she likes it.*

- *I look for maple trees to tap, when I go walking in the woods.*

- *When you work on your car outside you don't freeze.*

- *I would like to enlarge my home so my daughters would have more room, I would also like to fence in my entire yard so my dogs could run free.*

- *By the time I was sixteen I had earned quite a bit of money so I decided to buy a vehicle.*

- *My timing was just right, because if I had been a few minutes later I would have missed the most exciting miracle of my life.*

- *It does my heart good to know that there are still people, who dare to be different.*

PART VI -- ADDITIONAL THINGS YOU SHOULD KNOW

Much of the power you gain in developing the ability to recognize clauses and to understand "clause and effect" comes from learning to focus your message. When you can recognize the structure of the clauses and sentences you've used to convey your message, you begin to see the choices you have that allow you not only to correct the grammar and punctuation in your sentences but also to sharpen the focus of your message or to change it altogether. Without clear and proper focus, the most grammatically correct writing can still confuse, discourage, mislead, or simply bore your reader.

This chapter deals with concepts that we've mentioned in passing in earlier chapters and with new tips for improving your clauses and sentences. When you've finished reading the chapter, you might want to take something you've written recently and analyze it to see if you've overlooked opportunities to improve the focus of your message.

Focusing on the real subject

Now that you know how to find your subjects, you should be able to focus your reader's attention on them immediately and forcefully. Remember that "*there is/are,*" "*there was/were.*" "*it is,*" and "*it was*" constructions, though useful, throw the real subject of a sentence out of its rightful place and add to the wordiness of your text. Be sure not to rely on these constructions when they aren't called for.

Example:

There <u>were</u> three <u>children</u> standing on the corner.

Choice #1: You may leave the sentence as it is if your intent is to focus on the number of children rather than on the fact that they were standing on the corner.

Choice #2: If your intent is to focus on what the subject was doing, then you will want to put the real subject in its rightful place and turn the modifying gerund *"standing"* into a working verb.

Three children stood on the corner.

Making the most of your "voice"

How you use verbs in your clauses determines how focused your reader will be on both your subject and the actions or states of being you're trying to convey.

<u>Voice</u>

Clauses are most forceful and direct in English when they are in the active voice.

- A clause is in the active voice when the subject is the doer of the action.
- A clause is in the passive voice when the subject is the person, place, or thing being acted upon in the clause. The passive voice is marked by the use of the verb *"to be"* as an auxiliary.

Active Voice

The <u>man</u> <u>scolded</u> the boy for breaking the vase.

The independent clause is in the active voice: The subject *"man"* is the <u>doer</u> of the action *"scolded."*

Conversion from Active to Passive Voice

- For a clause to be convertible from the active voice to the passive voice, the receiver of the action must be known or knowable.
- In the passive voice, the <u>receiver</u> of the action (i.e., the direct object) becomes the subject, the auxiliary verb *"to be"* in the appropriate tense is added to the participle of the working verb, and the subject becomes the object of the preposition *"by"* or is omitted altogether.

The clause *"The man scolded the boy"* can be converted to the passive voice because the verb *"scolded"* has a direct object: *"boy"* (scolded whom? the boy). To convert it, we simply take the direct object, make it the subject of the sentence, add the verb *"to be"* as an auxiliary to the working verb, and make the doer of the action the object of the preposition *"by"* or omit him altogether:

The <u>boy</u> <u>was scolded</u> by the man for breaking the vase.

The <u>boy</u> <u>was scolded</u> for breaking the vase.

The clause is now in the passive voice because the subject *"boy"* is the <u>receiver</u> of the action *"scolded"* (i.e., the boy is the one being scolded).

Passive Voice

The woman was congratulated for her efforts.

The independent clause in this sentence space is in the passive voice because the subject "*woman*" is the <u>receiver</u> of the action "*congratulated*" (notice the use of the verb "*was*" as an auxiliary).

Conversion from Passive to Active Voice

- For a clause to be convertible from the passive voice to the active voice, the <u>doer</u> of the action must be known or knowable.
- In the active voice, the doer becomes the subject, the auxiliary verb "*to be*" is dropped and the working verb is put in the appropriate tense, and the subject becomes the <u>receiver</u> of the action.

To convert this clause to the active voice, you would have to know who did the congratulating. If you are not the author of this clause and don't know who the doer of the action was, you cannot convert the clause. However, if you know, for example, that the mayor was the one who did the action, you could convert the clause by making the doer the subject, eliminating the auxiliary, and making the "*woman*" the receiver of the action (i.e., the object of the verb):

The <u>mayor</u> <u>congratulated</u> the woman for her efforts.

The independent clause in this sentence is in the active voice because the subject "*mayor*" is the <u>doer</u> of the action "*congratulated.*"

Note: A clause is in neither voice when the working verb is a linking verb (e.g., the verb "*to be*" or any other verb that represents a state of being) and does not represent an action.

Choices

Once you understand voice, you are equipped to make additional choices to be sure your message is conveyed effectively and concisely.

Example:

The table was broken by one of the directors during the late session.

As you can see, there is only one clause in this sentence.

You may leave the sentence as it is if you wish, especially if you want to focus on the table. However, you have other choices, depending on your intent.

Choice #1 – You can convert this sentence to the active voice to make it more forceful and less wordy:

One of the directors broke the table during the late session.

Choice #2 – You can keep the sentence in the passive voice but eliminate the doer if you want to avoid casting blame.

The table was broken during the late session.

The passive voice is always wordier than the active voice. However, in determining conciseness, remember that purpose and message dictate how many words you should use. Don't make the mistake of assuming that using the fewest words is always the best choice.

Making use of time dimension

Because the verb is such an important part of a clause, your understanding of how verbs work is critical to your being able to harness the power of "clause and effect."

Simple and Perfect Tenses

Most people are familiar with the simple verb tenses -- past, present, and future – but many no longer seem to understand the function of the perfect tenses -- past perfect, present perfect, and future perfect.

- The simple tenses allow us to express actions or states of being that occur at a given moment in time.
- On the other hand, the perfect tenses, marked by the use of the various forms of the verb "*have*" as an auxiliary, add dimension to our communication by allowing us to write about two or more actions, at least one of which occurred, is occurring, or will occur before, up to, or after the action or actions expressed in a simple tense. Without the perfect tenses, we'd be unable to convey that sense of depth in our writing where time is concerned.

For example, in the following sentence, the past perfect tense allows us to indicate that the little girl ate <u>before</u> the mother left for work.

Satisfied that the little girl had already eaten, the mother left for work.

Now consider this sentence:

Since you took charge, the company became the top-rated medical consulting firm in the state.

Both verbs are in the simple past (*took* & *became*). However, the use of "since" indicates that the state of "becoming" occurred after the action of "taking charge" and is intended to span a period up to the present. This dimension cannot be conveyed without the use of the perfect tense – in this case, the present perfect.

Since you took charge, the company has become the top-rated medical consulting firm in the state.

If you can recognize within your clauses the working verbs and their tenses, you can choose tenses that add depth to your writing.

The progressive form of verbs

Another way of adding time dimension to your writing is through the use of the progressive form. This form, marked by the use of an "-ing" ending and the verb "to be" as an auxiliary, allows you to express actions or states of being that are in progress.

The boy is eating his dinner.

The girl was eating hers an hour ago.

They will both be eating their desserts an hour from now.

However, if you drag the reader unnecessarily through actions in progress, you'll make your writing more tedious and less concise that it should be.

Example:

We were walking hand in hand through the mall, and then we stopped for an ice cream.

There's usually no need to drag the reader through an action in progress. Let the "-*ing*" ending be a visual reminder to check for the unnecessary use of the progressive form.

Choice #1 – You can simply eliminate the progressive form from the first clause.

We walked hand in hand through the mall, and then we stopped for an ice cream.

Choice #2 – You can then subordinate one of the clauses to indicate where you want the reader to focus.

After we walked hand in hand through the mall, we stopped for an ice cream.

Choice #3 – Alternatively, you can now substitute a gerund for the subordinate clause to make the main idea more forceful.

After walking hand in hand through the mall, we stopped for an ice cream.

The progressive form is overused and should be avoided unless the progressive nature of the action is an important part of your message.

Writing more concisely

Avoiding verb/verbal pile-ups

When choosing a word to serve as the working verb of a clause, select a verb that

- best represents the real action you intend to convey, and
- requires the fewest number of infinitives to follow it.

Anytime you see a verb/verbal pile-up, ask yourself what the subject is really doing and simplify your clause by selecting the most appropriate verb possible. Often, you'll find the best verb suggested in the verbal you've used after the weak working verb.

Example:

The snowstorm will start to wind down tonight, and the winds will begin to decrease shortly thereafter.

In this compound sentence (two independent clauses within one sentence space), both clauses make use of weak verbs. How can you tell? The presence of infinitives (*"to"* plus a verbal) after the working verbs should set off an alarm that tells you to reevaluate your verb to be sure it is as precise as possible.

In the first clause, what will the storm do tonight? Apparently, it will "*start*" to do something. Is "*start*" a good choice as a working verb? To answer this, look at the infinitive that follows it: "*to wind down.*" The action of winding down is, by definition, a progressive action that is accomplished over a period of time. Do we need to use "*start*" to get the idea across to the reader that the storm will become weaker over a period of time? No we don't, because such a progressive action is implied by the verb "*wind down,*" which, in any case, represents the real action the subject is about to do. The clause is less wordy and more forceful if it simply states:

The <u>snowstorm</u> <u>will wind down</u> tonight,

The same principle applies to the second clause. The verb "*begin*" is useless because "*decrease*" implies a progressive action that is accomplished over a period of time and represents the real action to be done by the subject. This clause would be improved if it simply stated:

and the <u>winds</u> <u>will decrease</u> shortly thereafter.

The resulting sentence is more concise and direct and, therefore, more forceful:

The <u>snowstorm</u> <u>will wind down</u> tonight, and the <u>winds</u> <u>will decrease</u> shortly thereafter.

Eliminating unnecessary clauses

Your ability to locate clauses can also help you to simplify your writing and attack your subject directly. No more beating around the bush, please!

Example:

Another _problem_ _which_ _I feel_ greatly _affects_ my writing capabilities _is_ the anxiety I _feel_ when having to write.

If we eliminate the dependent clauses that simply tell the reader what "I feel" and recognize that the independent clause is purely descriptive, we can focus on the real subject and the real verb to come up with a much more concise and direct sentence.

Anxiety greatly _affects_ my ability to write.

Just think of the money you'd save on stationery or E-mail time if you could reduce all your sentences in this way.

Using modifiers wisely

One of the best tools in achieving conciseness is an understanding of the elements as your disposal that can serve as modifiers:

- Clauses (independent and dependent) that express states of being (verb "to be")
- Relative clauses (dependent clauses that begin with "that," "who," "which"...)
- Words, phrases, or clauses set in apposition
- Phrases (prepositional, verbal,...)
- Possessives (nouns, pronouns)
- Verbals (participles, gerunds)
- Adjectives and adverbs
- Nouns that describe other nouns

You can work your way down from whole clauses to single words or up from single words to whole clauses to get your message across as effectively as possible.

- The direction you take depends on how much emphasis you wish to give to the modifier. If the modifying idea you wish to express needs little emphasis, you work your way down to the most concise modifier you can find. If the idea needs greater emphasis, you work your way up to the appropriate level of emphasis, remembering that a single independent clause carries the most emphasis (i.e., 100% of the emphasis within a sentence space).

Using one of the examples used throughout this book, you'll see the choices this knowledge affords you:

Example:

The car that was towed out of the parking lot belonged to Paul.

In this sentence, we notice a relative clause: "*that was towed out of the parking lot.*" We recognize that we could reduce this modifying clause to a verbal (participial) phrase: "*towed out of the parking lot.*" This change allows us to eliminate two words and a clause and create a more powerful simple sentence:

The car towed out of the parking lot belonged to Paul.

Here's the original sentence with a change of subordination.

Example:

The car that belonged to Paul was towed out of the parking lot.

In this sentence, the relative clause -- *"that belonged to Paul"* -- is a modifying clause and could be reduced to a verbal (gerundial) phrase -- *"belonging to Paul"* -- or, even more drastically, to a possessive noun -- *"Paul's."*

The car belonging to Paul was towed out of the parking lot.
or

Paul's car was towed out of the parking lot.

Certainly, unless there's a reason to stress the modifier, the last example is the most forceful and the most concise option.

Varying the structure of your sentences

Your ability to spot clauses gives you the ability to understand the types of sentences you've created. This, in turn, provides you with choices that can impact the clarity and style with which you convey your intended meaning to the reader.

When little children tell stories or relate incidents, they rely very heavily on simple and compound sentences to express themselves:

Yesterday was my birthday, and my sister went to the store, and she bought me a present. She came home, and I looked in the bag, and I saw a big pad of paper and a new pencil. I was very happy, and I kissed her, and I ran to my room with my new things.

As you'll note, none of the ideas is subordinated (that is, there are no dependent clauses); all are presented as if they were equally important.

- This lack of subordination not only sounds elementary, but it also denies readers any help in determining the relative importance of the ideas presented.
- Readers must deal with and remember nine main ideas without being quite sure which of those ideas they are expected to focus on and give special attention to.

Read the following subordinated version, and see if the meanings and tone change at all.

Because yesterday was my birthday, my sister went to the store and bought me a present. When she came home, I looked in the bag and saw a big pad of paper and a new pencil. I was so happy that I kissed her. Then I ran to my room with my new things.

It is your job as a writer to provide your readers with clues as to the relative importance of the ideas you present and to help them see how those ideas interrelate.

- You can accomplish this by subordinating some of your ideas to the main concepts you're discussing and by varying your sentence style.

There are four major reasons why you should use different types of sentences and subordinate certain ideas when you write:

- Reason #1: To make clear how the ideas relate to each other (relationship)

Madame K's pizza is convenient for me; my home is only three blocks away.

Independent ideas, whether presented in simple or in compound sentences, stand alone. Their interrelationship with the ideas that precede or follow them is not made clear and sometimes not even implied. Appropriate conjunctions (coordinating and subordinate) can help to establish the right connections.

Madame K's pizza is convenient for me since [or because] my home is only three blocks away.

In this revision, you'll note that the reason the writer considers the business convenient (its location) is made clear to the reader.

- Reason #2: To make clear the relative degree of emphasis you wish to give your ideas (emphasis)

Example:

The innovative package is bulkier. It provides great advertising space. It protects the pizza from getting squashed in the middle.

All ideas come across as being of equal value and emphasis when presented in their own independent clauses. Subordinating some ideas by expressing them in dependent clauses or in phrases or compound constructions can help the reader to detect the emphasis you wish to give them.

Although the innovative package is bulkier, it provides great advertising space and protects the pizza from getting squashed in the middle.

In this revision, you'll note that the negative "*bulkier*" is subordinated while the other ideas are presented in a compound, or parallel, construction that makes it clear that they are perceived as being equal to each other in value. If the last idea merits greater emphasis, it can be set off as a separate sentence:

Although the innovative package is bulkier, it provides great advertising space. It also protects the pizza from getting squashed in the middle.

- Reason #3: To help the reader remember as many of the ideas you present as possible (organization)

Example:

I went to the mall the other day. I saw Jane Smith, an old neighbor. I saw John Goodall, a classmate. I also ran into Paul Tardif, another old neighbor of mine. It was like old-home week. I even ran into Sally Peters, another classmate, as I was leaving.

When you constantly bombard your readers with independent clauses, you overwhelm their natural capacity to remember individual items or ideas. If you understand that a human being's short term memory can handle only five or six items at a time, you begin to realize the problem you are creating for your readers. By helping them to sort out the information and to see how the items relate to each other, you are more likely to get them to remember the bulk of your message.

When I <u>went</u> to the mall the other day, I <u>ran</u> into two old neighbors of mine, Jane Smith and Paul Tardif, and two former classmates, John Goodall and Sally Peters. It <u>felt</u> like old-home week.

Be kind to your reader, and both you and your reader will reap the rewards of your kindness.

- Reason #4: To add meaningful variety and sophistication to your presentation (style)

As you saw in the first example used in this section, a child's writing sounds very elementary because only simple and compound sentences are used. You can guard against such a problem by varying the types of sentences you use.

- In most formal writing, especially in business and report writing, it is very important to maintain consistent focus on your subject throughout a paragraph of text to be sure that the reader understands your message.
- Unfortunately, such consistency can sometimes lead to repetition that might become distracting to the reader.

- Since only the main clauses of your sentences require such consistent attention to your subject, you can create variety by inverting complex sentences and by varying the types of sentences you use.

The overall result, of course, is to help the reader make sense of your total message (meaning).

Remember: Exercise your options and be sure your choices reflect your purpose, your message, and the needs of your reader.

PART VII - THE PAYOFF 2

Here are more examples of "clause and effect" in action:

Many household products which we are accustomed to using not only hurt us individually, but also as a whole are causing our planet to be filled with pollutants.

- Clause #1 – Many household <u>products</u> not only <u>hurt</u> us individually, but also as a whole <u>are</u> <u>causing</u> our planet to be filled with pollutants.
- Clause #2 – which <u>we</u> <u>are</u> accustomed to using

<u>Can you spot the choices?</u>

Choice #1: You could make the compound verbs in the main clause parallel (i.e., make them both progressive or both simple in form), which would improve the sound and flow of the sentence.

- *Many household products not only hurt us individually, but also as a whole cause our planet to be filled with pollutants.*

  or

- *Many household products are not only hurting us individually, but also as a whole are causing our planet to be filled with pollutants.*

Notwithstanding what was said earlier about using the progressive form, in this case the progressive form may be the best choice because it may have a greater impact on the reader than the static simple tense. A reader who connects with the ongoing problem that is the subject of this sentence may be more inclined to take the message to heart.

Choice #2: You could turn the modifying dependent clause (clause #2) into an adjective to make the sentence more concise.

- *Many commonly-used household products are not only hurting us individually, but also as a whole are causing our planet to be filled with pollutants.*

Choice #3: You could strengthen the sentence by finding the best verbs and eliminating any verbal pile-ups you encounter.

- *Many commonly-used household products are not only harming us individually, but also as a whole are polluting our planet.*

Choice #4 – You could improve the punctuation by isolating and repositioning the interrupting phrase "*as a whole.*"

- *Many commonly-used household products are not only harming us individually, but are also, as a whole, polluting our planet.*

Let's try another sentence:

I already have knowledge that most security departments have their dispatch offices located in their security buildings.

- Clause #1 – I already <u>have</u> knowledge
- Clause #2 – that most security <u>departments</u> <u>have</u> their dispatch offices located in their security buildings.

Do you see that both clauses use the same non-action verb?

Choice #1: You can choose a stronger verb for the first clause.

- *I already know*

Choice #2: You can do the same for the dependent clause.

- *that most security departments locate their dispatch offices in their security buildings.*

Choice #3: You can decide whether or not the fact that you know something is more important than what you know. If it is, then you can leave the sentence as it is. On the other hand, if the focus of your message belongs not on you but on what you know, then you can eliminate the first clause and create a new independent clause.

- *Most security departments locate their dispatch offices in their security buildings.*

Be aware that focusing on "I know" or "I think" or "I feel" is one of the easiest ways to weaken your writing, especially when it comes to business communications, formal reports, and persuasive writing.

<u>Here's another sentence:</u>

The proposed report that I will write on day care is an important issue nowadays.

- Clause #1 – The proposed <u>report</u> <u>is</u> an important issue nowadays
- Clause #2 – that <u>I</u> <u>will write</u> on day care

Do you see ways to improve this sentence? I hope you see that (a) the report is not an issue, (b) the independent clause is merely descriptive, and (c) writing "on" day care doesn't really make sense.

Choice #1: You can begin by identifying the important issue and making that the subject of the independent clause, at least for now.

- *Day care is an important issue nowadays*

Choice #2: You can then identify what "I" will write.

- *that I will write a report about*

Choice #3: You can now simplify the sentence by reducing the dependent clause to an adjective.

- *My report*

Choice #4: You can shift the ideas around to place the focus where it appears to belong.

- *My report will deal with day care, an important issue nowadays.*

There are obviously many other ways to edit this sentence, depending on your intended focus and the effect you want to create on your audience. Being able to spot the clauses is key to recognizing those choices.

Let's try a group of sentences this time.

On a talk show there were several lotto winners. They were interviewed. Each gave their own success story. They all gave accounts of how their lives had changed for the good and the bad.

- Clause #1 – On a talk show, there <u>were</u> several lotto <u>winners</u>.
- Clause #2 – <u>They</u> <u>were interviewed</u>.
- Clause #3 – <u>Each</u> <u>gave</u> their own success story.
- Clause #4 – <u>They</u> all <u>gave</u> accounts of
- Clause #5 – how their <u>lives</u> <u>were changed</u> for the good and the bad. (Note that this is the only dependent clause in this group of sentences.)

Although independent clauses expressed in simple sentences can be very forceful, a consecutive series of such sentences may indicate a failure to subordinate ideas and to focus on real subjects and verbs.

Choice #1: If you recognize that the purpose of the first sentence is simply to identify the subject being focused on, you can begin to rewrite this series of sentences by putting the subject in its rightful place and looking for a verb in the sentences that follow.

- *On a talk show, several lotto winners*

Choice #2: You can now merge this with the second sentence.

- *On a talk show, several lotto winners were interviewed.*

Choice #3: You can then look at the next sentences to see if they can be merged as well. What you find is that "success story" doesn't quite make sense if the accounts include the bad changes, so perhaps that's where the merging can take place. (You will also want to correct the agreement error that has been created by using the singular pronoun *"each"* with the plural adjective *"their."*)

- *They gave their own accounts of how their lives had changed for the good and the bad.*

Choice #4: In this series of sentences, the real subject appears to be *"several lotto winners"* and the focus of the message appears to be what they told the audience. Everything else should be subordinated to that main message.

- *During a talk show interview, several lotto winners gave accounts of how their lives had changed, both for the good and for the bad, as a result of their luck.*

Let's try another group of sentences:

I go to my cousin's house. Sometimes she makes lasagna. Lasagna is my favorite meal.

As you can see, all three sentences are simple and contain only one clause.

Choice #1: You can establish a connection between the first two sentences by showing how they are related.

- *When I go to my cousin's house, she sometimes makes lasagna.*

Choice #2: Since the third sentence is merely descriptive, we know that it can be either subordinated or replaced by a modifier or modifying phrase.

- *When I go to my cousin's house, she sometimes makes lasagna, my favorite meal.*

<u>Here are additional analyses that should strengthen your understanding of what's been discussed in this text:</u>

I <u>had</u> drapes made for the picture window by a professional seamstress, <u>they</u> <u>are</u> fully insulated on the back side for warmth in the winter months.

In this sentence, the subject/verb combinations have been underlined. Your analysis should reveal to you that both clauses are independent since they can both stand alone and include no subordinating terms. Knowing this, you should recognize that the sentence is not correctly punctuated and contains a run-on error. The sentence should read:

- *I <u>had</u> drapes made for the picture window by a professional seamstress; <u>they</u> <u>are</u> fully insulated on the back side for warmth in the winter months.*

However, an ability to locate your subjects and verbs not only clarifies punctuation problems but provides you with choices about how to express the message itself.

You might begin by noticing, for instance, that the two independent subjects within this single sentence ("*I*" and "*they*") are different. The reader's focus has been shifted from one idea to another within one sentence.

- Could this shift be avoided?
- Could avoiding such a shift strengthen the sentence?

Notice, too, that the verbs are weak and do not represent actions.

- Is the first part of the message really that I "*had*" something?
- Is it worth giving the second idea, which is merely descriptive, 50% of the emphasis of this sentence space? Could this clause be subordinated to the first? Could it be changed to express more than mere description?

Here are some possible choices:

Choice #1:

- *I hired a professional seamstress to make fully insulated drapes for the picture window. These drapes block out the cold in the winter months.*

Choice #2:

- *The _drapes_ that _I hired_ a professional seamstress to make for the picture window _are_ fully insulated on the back side for warmth in the winter months.*

Even if you ultimately decide to leave the sentences as they are, you'll benefit from knowing the options you have at hand. Your message will be the product of conscious choice, not of random wording.

Here's another example:

Our _family_ _enjoys_ apple picking. _We_ _made_ a fun game out of it. When _we_ _arrived_ at the apple orchard _I_ _made_ a bet with them. The _person_ _who_ _finds_ the biggest and reddest apple _will receive_ five dollars.

In this group of sentences, I've once again underlined the subject/verb combinations. If you are able to identify the types of clauses, you should see that a commaa is missing in the third sentence, which begins with a dependent clause. You should also see that a colon could be used to separate the last two sentences since one leads into or points to the other.

Your ability to spot subjects and verbs should also make clear to you the inconsistency in verb tenses. Notice the inexplicable shift from present to past to present again before using the future tense. Consistency immediately improves the paragraph:

- *Our family enjoys apple picking. We make a fun game out of it. When we arrive at the apple orchard, I make a bet with everyone: The person who finds the biggest and reddest apple will receive five dollars.*

Once the basic sentences have been corrected, you can now focus on the types of sentences used. The first two sentences are simple sentences that share a common subject.

Choice: You could link the sentences through subordination to improve the message and make the writing seem less elementary.

- *Our family enjoys apple picking because we make a fun game out of it. When we arrive at the apple orchard, I make a bet with everyone: The person who finds the biggest and reddest apple will receive five dollars.*

Now we can see a connection that was not clearly expressed before. That's what subordination is all about.

<u>Let's try another.</u>

<u>I wanted</u> to attend college to earn my degree. Most importantly, to better myself as a person. Also to enhance my academic skills. <u>I would like</u> to pursue some courses in Art also.

As you can see, neither the second nor the third sentence space in this group of sentences contains a subject/verb combination, which means they are both fragments.

Choice #1: Some people might think that these fragments emphasize the separate items listed. However, if you list these items within the first sentence, in an order that makes sense and builds in importance, you can actually create a more powerful presentation.

- *I wanted to attend college to enhance my academic skills, to earn my degree, and, most importantly, to better myself as a person. I would like to pursue some courses in Art also.*

Choice #2: Next, you've probably noticed the inconsistency in verb tenses between the first and the second sentences. There's too big a jump from the past to the conditional future. This can easily be corrected, either by using the past tense throughout, or by using the present tense to connect to the conditional future.

- *I wanted to attend college to enhance my academic skills, to earn my degree, and, most importantly, to better myself as a person. I wanted to pursue some courses in Art also.*

  or

- *I want to attend college to enhance my academic skills, to earn my degree, and, most importantly, to better myself as a person. I would like to pursue some courses in Art also.*

Choice #3: Finally, you probably recognize that "*also*" is out of place. It must either be set off by a comma or put in its proper place.

- *I wanted to attend college to enhance my academic skills, to earn my degree, and, most importantly, to better myself as a person. I also wanted to pursue some courses in Art.*

CHALLENGE

If you'd like additional practice, see if you can edit the following sentences to make them as correct and as effective as possible. You'll find suggested editing choices in Appendix D.

1. *There is really very few reasons not to further your education.*
2. *To do this recommendation will involve three basic steps.*
3. *I like Natanis; for it is a very small campground.*
4. *Young people, who dye and or spike their hair, are only trying to express themselves.*
5. *The v-seal is not staying in place and in some situations have come completely off.*
6. *I love to visit with my grandmother, to me she is the greatest relative I have.*
7. *We are adding your name to our mailing list, therefore, you do not need to make a second request.*
8. *I went home with all my family and we went out to dinner, of course it was on me.*
9. *Procedures done in a hospital setting I like to see done correctly.*

<u>Note</u>: These sentences are not the simple, grammatically correct sentences you normally encounter as examples in grammar workbooks. Rather, they were written by students in my writing classes, as were almost all of the examples in this text, and reflect the complexities that many people encounter in trying to revise their own writing and the writing of others. Good luck!

CONCLUSION

As I mentioned at the beginning, this text was not meant to be an exhaustive treatment of the subject of grammar, nor was it intended to replace traditional grammar texts. What I hoped to accomplish was to focus on a process that, in my opinion, is most crucial to the development of editing skills – i.e., the ability to recognize clauses – and to help you see how that ability can have an effect on your editing skills. I also hoped to instill in you a desire to learn more about the entire language process itself.

I remember the joy my students experienced whenever they acquired new skills in language, and the satisfaction they voiced whenever those skills paid off for them. I wish you the same joy and satisfaction as you develop your mastery of "Clause and Effect."

APPENDIX A

Commonly used pronouns, prepositions, and conjunctions

The following lists are provided to give you a sense of the types of words you should be looking for. A search of grammar texts or Internet resources should allow you to find more extensive lists of prepositions and subordinating conjunctions.

Pronouns

- Personal: I, you, he, she, it, we, you, they, me, him, her, us, them
- Relative: That, which, who, whoever, whomever
- Demonstrative: This, that, these, those

Coordinating conjunctions

- And, or, nor, for, so, but, yet

Subordinating conjunctions (these types of words are followed by a subject/verb combination and related words)

- Because, when, where, why, before, after, if, as if, since, though, till, unless, whenever, wherever, until...

Prepositions (these types of words are followed by nouns and their modifiers)

- In, on, under, around, before, after, over, under, for, by, with, above, below, within, without...

SUZANNE R. ROY

APPENDIX B

A quick review of the Subject/Verb Identification Process

Step 1.

Scan the entire sentence and identify all relative and demonstrative pronouns. (If you find none, go to step 2.)

- If the relative or demonstrative pronoun is followed immediately by a verb, underline it as a subject.
- If the relative or demonstrative pronoun is followed immediately by a noun or a pronoun, cross it out since it cannot be a subject.

Step 2.

Go back to the beginning of the sentence and scan the sentence backwards from the first noun or personal pronoun you find.

- If no object-creator precedes the first noun or personal pronoun you've identified, underline the word.
- If you find an object-creator, cross out the noun or pronoun and search for the next noun or personal pronoun in the sentence. Keep doing this until you've found the first noun or pronoun you can underline, and go on to Step 3.

Step 3.

Apply the scanning process in Step 2 to all the remaining nouns (including gerunds and infinitives that serve as nouns) and personal pronouns you encounter in the rest of the sentence.

If you reach an object-creator, ask "whom" or "what" (or "when," "where," or "to whom" to find indirect objects) after that word.

- If your answer is the single noun or pronoun whose function you are trying to identify, that noun or pronoun is an object, so cross it out.
- If the answer to the question you ask after an object-creator is a group of words of which the noun or pronoun is a part, then the single noun or pronoun is not an object and must be a subject. Underline it. (For example, in the sentence "*It took a while before he discovered you were gone,*" "*you*" is preceded by an object-creator – the verb "*discovered*" – but is not the object of that verb. What "*he discovered*" is not "*you*" but "[that] *you were gone.*" Had the relative pronoun "*that*" not been suppressed, it would have served as a barrier that would have made it evident that "*you*" must be a subject.)
- If you reach any one of the barriers listed below before coming across an object-creator, stop your search and assume that your noun or pronoun is a subject. Underline the word and move on to the next noun or pronoun.

Barriers to watch for:

- A subordinating conjunction (see list in Appendix A)
- A relative pronoun that you've already crossed out
- The capital letter that marks the beginning of the sentence you're analyzing
- A period or semicolon or any sentence-ending punctuation

Step 4.

Once you've completed the process of identifying all the possible subjects in your sentence, ask what those subjects are doing or being within the sentence, and you'll find the working verbs that they are linked to. These subject/verb combinations are called clauses.

APPENDIX C

Answers to the Punctuation Challenge

- *Spring is the most exciting season of the year for me because I think of it as a time of renewal.* [Independent clause *dependent clause*]

- *I like riding through the White Mountains to see the view; it's simply breathtaking.*[Independent clause + semicolon + independent clause]

- *We pack everything in the pick-up and drive to every brook we can find.* [Independent clause *dependent clause* - Note: *"We pack...and drive"* is a compound verb within a single clause. Had this group of words included two subjects – i.e., *"We pack everything in the pick-up, and we drive to every brook..."* – the two resulting independent clauses would have required special punctuation to avoid a run-on error.)

- *I can't ice skate, but I sometimes go with my girlfriend because she likes it.* [Independent clause + comma and coordinating conjunction + independent clause *dependent clause*]

- *I look for maple trees to tap when I go walking in the woods.* [Independent clause *dependent clause*]

- *When you work on your car outside, you don't freeze.* [*Dependent clause* + comma + independent clause]

- *I would like to enlarge my home so my daughters would have more room. I would also like to fence in my entire yard so my dogs could run free.* [Independent clause *dependent clause* + period + independent clause *dependent clause*]

- *By the time I was sixteen, I had earned quite a bit of money, so I decided to buy a vehicle.* [*Dependent clause* + comma + independent clause + comma and coordinating conjunction + independent clause]

- *My timing was just right because, if I had been a few minutes later, I would have missed the most exciting miracle of my life.* [Independent clause *1st dependent clause (partial)* + comma + *interrupting 2nd dependent clause* + comma + *rest of 1st dependent clause*]

- *It does my heart good to know that there are still people who dare to be different.* [Independent clause *dependent clause dependent clause*]

APPENDIX D

Answers to the CHALLENGE

1. There *is* really very few <u>reasons</u> not to further your education.

The sentence space contains a single independent clause. – No additional punctuation is needed.

"*There*" delays the real subject (*reasons*). – However, since the intent of this sentence appears to be to point to the number of "*reasons not to further your education,*" the construction can remain as it is.

Since the verb "*to be*" is used (*is*), "*there*" and "*reasons*" equate, which means that "*there*" should be considered to be plural like "*reasons.*" – The singular verb (*is*) does not match its plural subject.

- *There are really very few reasons not to further your education.*

2. <u>To do</u> this recommendation <u>will involve</u> three basic steps.

The sentence space contains a single independent clause. – No additional punctuation is needed.

The subject (the infinitive verbal *to do*) sounds awkward because you don't usually "do" a recommendation and because an infinitive usually sounds more awkward than a gerund (*doing*) when used as a subject. – If a verbal is to be used as the subject, it should reflect the meaning of the sentence.

Choice #1:

- *To carry out this recommendation will involve three basic steps.*

Choice #2:

- *Carrying out this recommendation will involve three basic steps.*

3. **I *like* Natanis; for *it* *is* a very small campground.**

This sentence contains two independent clauses. – Although *"for"* can appear to mean "because," here it can be considered a coordinating conjunction. As such, it should be preceded by a comma, not a semicolon, because it joins two independent clauses.

Choice #1:

- *I like Natanis, for it is a very small campground.*

Since the use of *"for"* in this way can sound a bit formal and even archaic, you may want to use the subordinating conjunction "because" instead.

Choice #2:

- *I like Natanis because it is a very small campground.*

4. **Young *people, who dye* or *spike* their hair, *are* only *trying* to express themselves.**

This sentence contains one independent clause and one dependent clause. – Although the dependent clause has been inserted into the independent clause, it is an essential clause and does not warrant the use of extra punctuation.

Choice:

- *Young people who dye or spike their hair are only trying to express themselves.*

5. **The *v-seal* *is* not *staying* in place and in some situations *have come* completely *off*.**

This sentence contains one independent clause. However, a non-essential phrase (*in some situations*) has been inserted into the clause and should be set off by commas.

Choice #1:

- *The v-seal is not staying in place and, in some situations, have come completely off.*

The subject of the main clause (*v-seal*) is singular, but the second verb that relates to it (*have exhausted*) is plural.

Choice #2:

- *The v-seal is not staying in place and, in some situations, has come completely off.*

The two working verbs in this sentence are not in the same form. One is in the progressive form, and one is a perfect tense. Since neither the progressive form nor the perfect tense is necessary in this sentence, the use of simple tenses is advisable.

Choice #3:

- *The v-seal does not stay in place and, in some situations, comes off completely.*

6. *I love* to visit with my grandmother, to me *she is* the greatest relative [that] *I have*.

This sentence contains two independent clauses and one dependent clause. – A comma by itself is not strong enough to link two independent clauses, so there is a run-on error within the sentence space. Since the second statement is meant to be important, it should probably occupy its own sentence space.

Choice:

- *I love to visit my grandmother. To me, she is the greatest relative I have.*

7. *We are adding* your name to our mailing list, therefore, *you do* not *need* to make a second request.

This sentence contains two independent clauses. – If you use an adverb to link two independent clauses, it should be preceded by a semicolon and followed by a comma.

Choice #1:

- *We are adding your name to our mailing list; therefore, you do not need to make a second request.*

Because the progressive form (*are adding*) is not really necessary, you may want to consider using the perfect tense instead:

Choice #2:

- *We have added your name to our mailing list; therefore, you will not need to make a second request.*

To strengthen the relationship between the two ideas, you may want to subordinate one of the ideas and turn this compound sentence into a complex sentence instead.

Choice #3:

- *Because we have added your name to our mailing list, you will not need to make a second request.*

If you want to focus on the reader, you may want to change the subject and voice of the dependent clause.

Choice #4:

- *Because your name has been added to our mailing list, you will not need to make a second request.*

8. **<u>I went</u> home with all my family and <u>we went</u> out to dinner, of course <u>it was</u> on me.**

This sentence contains three independent clauses. – When a coordinating conjunction (*and*) is used to link independent clauses, it must be preceded by a comma. Also, if you use an adverb (*of course*) to link two independent clauses, it should be preceded by a semicolon and followed by a comma. These mistakes are all run-on errors.

Choice #1:

- *I went home with all my family, and we went out to dinner; of course, it was on me.*

Remembering that a series of independent clauses may signal a failure either to subordinate or to merge related ideas, you may want to be clearer about how the ideas being expressed relate to each other.

Choice #2:

- *When I went home with all my family, we went out to dinner; of course, it was on me.*

"*It*" in the last clause has no antecedent.

Choice #3:

- *When I went home with all my family, we went out to dinner; of course, the meal was on me.*

Looking at the subjects in this sentence (*I, we, meal*), we find no consistency or sustained focus. You could merge the ideas to make the subjects more parallel and the sentence more concise.

Choice #4:

- *When I went home with all my family, I treated them to dinner.*

However, if paying for the meal is the item you want to stress, then consider sticking with the original second clause (*we went out to dinner*) but placing the final clause in a sentence space of its own:

Choice #5:

- *When I went home with all my family, we went out to dinner. Of course, the meal was on me.*

9. Procedures done in a hospital setting I like to see done correctly.

There is only one independent clause in this sentence. You may have noticed that the sentence sounds awkward because the object of the verb comes before the verb. The sentence could be improved simply by placing the subject and verb in their normal place.

Choice #1:

- *I like to see procedures done in a hospital setting done correctly.*

You may also have noticed that the first "*done*" is not a working verb but a participle (a verbal). Since participles function as modifiers, you have the choice of reducing the entire phrase "*done in a hospital setting*" to a single word.

Choice #2:

- *I like to see hospital procedures done correctly.*

You might also want to change the second *"done"* to a more appropriate verbal.

Choice #3:

- *I like to see hospital procedures performed correctly.*

Finally, depending on your intent and your audience, you might want to make *"procedures"* your subject.

Choice #4:

- *Hospital procedures must be performed correctly.*

ABOUT THE AUTHOR

Suzanne R. Roy earned her Master's Degree in English from the University of Maine in Orono and taught basic and business writing for several years in the University of Maine system. She wrote *"La Bonne Aventure,"* a bilingual children's television series, and is a member of The Dramatists Guild of America. Two of her one-act plays - *Tradition* and *Caretakers* – were performed and won awards in Australia. She was also a contributor to the book *Inspiring Creativity,* an anthology of articles by creativity coaches from around the country.

Suzanne is currently a self-employed business consultant and uses her writing and editing skills on a regular basis. *Understanding CLAUSE AND EFFECT* is the first in a series of writing texts that she anticipates making available within the next year or two.